Songs of the Church
by William Bullock

Address:
HardPress
8345 NW 66TH ST #2561
MIAMI FL 33166-2626
USA
Email: info@hardpress.net

SONGS OF THE CHURCH.

BY

REV. WILLIAM BULLOCK,

HALIFAX, NOVA SCOTIA.

"Sing us one of the Songs of Zion."
PSALM cxxxvii.

HALIFAX:
PRINTED FOR THE AUTHOR.
1854.

DAVID CLAPP.....PRINTER.

TO

HIS GRACE THE PRESIDENT

AND TO

THE OFFICERS AND MEMBERS

OF

The Society for the Propagation of the
Gospel in Foreign Parts,

THESE

SONGS OF THE CHURCH

ARE

RESPECTFULLY DEDICATED

BY

THEIR DEVOTED PRESBYTER AND MISSIONARY,

WILLIAM BULLOCK.

PREFACE.

THESE " Psalms and Hymns and Spiritual Songs " were written amidst the various scenes of Missionary life, and intended to promote the work of piety in which the Missionary is engaged; and they are dedicated to the Great Missionary Society which has been the Vanguard of the English Church, in all the colonies of the English Crown. It is not in the vain expectation that the volume will exalt the Society, or spread her renown, but, that the Author may express his own admiration of the true catholic spirit, with which, in the most difficult times, she has conducted her noble enterprise; and the grateful sense which he entertains of the care with which she provides both for the usefulness and the comfort of her Missionaries, one of whom he has been for thirty-two years.

During that time the Author has seen the work of the Society increase with amazing rapidity, and

1*

although public sympathy and public liberality have not kept pace with her zeal, she has steadily pursued her course through good and evil report, extending the Episcopate to all the habitable parts of the empire, and girdling the whole earth with a belt of evangelical glory.

These Songs of the Church are written and arranged for private and domestic use, to aid our fellow-Christians who have settled in our new countries, and are deprived of the stated services of the sanctuary; and it is hoped that, by connecting the subject of the Hymn with these services, they may at once promote sound piety, and keep alive and cherish an affection for the Church.

To render them more generally useful, the Author has endeavored to preserve as much simplicity as possible. He hopes, however, that he has not adopted a phraseology unworthy of the subject, or which may, in any manner, offend the taste and judgment of the well-educated reader.

HALIFAX, NOVA SCOTIA,
July, 1854.

CONTENTS.

PART I.

CONTENTS.

9

Seventh Sunday after Trinity 115
Eighth Sunday after Trinity 116
Ninth Sunday after Trinity.   No. 1 117
Ninth Sunday after Trinity.   No. 2 119
Tenth Sunday after Trinity 120
Eleventh Sunday after Trinity 121
Twelfth Sunday after Trinity 122
Thirteenth Sunday after Trinity 123
Fourteenth Sunday after Trinity.   No. 1 125
Fourteenth Sunday after Trinity.   No. 2 126
Fifteenth Sunday after Trinity.   No. 1 128
Fifteenth Sunday after Trinity.   No. 2—After an unproductive harvest 129
Fifteenth Sunday after Trinity.   No. 3 130
Sixteenth Sunday after Trinity 132
Seventeenth Sunday after Trinity 133
Eighteenth Sunday after Trinity 135
Nineteenth Sunday after Trinity 136
Twentieth Sunday after Trinity 138
Twenty-first Sunday after Trinity 139
Twenty-second Sunday after Trinity 141
Twenty-third Sunday after Trinity 142
Twenty-fourth Sunday after Trinity 143
Sunday next before Advent 145
St. Andrew's Day 146
St. Thomas the Apostle 147
Conversion of St. Paul.   No. 1 149
Conversion of St. Paul.   No. 2 150
Presentation of Christ in the Temple 151
St. Matthias's Day 152
The Annunciation of the Blessed Virgin Mary . . . 153
St. Mark's Day 155
St. Philip and St. James's Day 156
St. Barnabas the Apostle 158
St. John Baptist's Day.   No. 1 159
St. John Baptist's Day.   No. 2 160
St. Peter's Day 162
St. James the Apostle 163
St. Bartholomew the Apostle 165
St. Matthew the Apostle 166
St. Michael and all Angels.   No. 1 167
St. Michael and all Angels.   No. 2 169
St. Luke the Evangelist 171
St. Simon and St. Jude 172
All Saints' Day.   No. 1 173
All Saints' Day.   No. 2 174

CONTENTS.

PART II.

PART I.

SONGS OF THE CHURCH

FOR

ALL THE SUNDAYS AND HOLYDAYS IN THE YEAR.

SONGS OF THE CHURCH.

FIRST SUNDAY IN ADVENT. No. 1.

"The night is far spent, the day is at hand; let us therefore cast off the works of darkness, and let us put on the armour of light." Rom. xiii. 12.

On Thee, whose glory fills the sky,
O Christ, our Saviour, we rely,
   And adoration yield:
In darken'd scenes, and midst the blaze
Of cloudless noon in summer days,
   Thou art our Sun and Shield.

Our sun, in whose effulgent ray
The darkest night is turned to day,
   Transparent "*light of light:*"
Our shield, on Thy extended arm,
Thy trusting saints shall fear no harm,
   Protected by Thy might.

2

The night is passing fast away,
And earth is ting'd with coming day ;
   "'Tis high time to awake :"
'T is time the deeds of night to shun,
To pray for light, and watch the sun,
   Until the morning break.

Though earth dissolve, and like a scroll
Of flame, the heavens together roll,
   Thy promise shall prevail :
Amidst the universal shock,
Hope our sure anchor on the rock,
   The rock within the vail.

With no more war, and no more night,
Released from foes to walk in light,
   With Thy redeem'd above :
And, through our never-ending days,
To see Thy face and sing Thy praise,
   And dwell with Thee in love.

FIRST SUNDAY IN ADVENT. No. 2.

THE night, that on the mountains spread
Its gloom, is passing fast away,
And earth, as rising from the dead,
Is fringèd with the morning ray.

On error's path, with healing wing,
The Sun of Righteousness shall rise,
'Wake, tenants of the dust, and sing,
And let your anthems fill the skies.

O Saviour Christ, with love and fear,
We wait Thy coming steps to greet,
For now is our salvation near ;
Make us for this salvation meet.

O let Thy glory round us shine,
And from our hearts dispel the night ;
Pour down Thy rays of grace divine,
And flood the world with living light.

SECOND SUNDAY IN ADVENT. No. 1.

"Whatsoever things were written aforetime, were written for our learning, that we, through patience and comfort of the scriptures, might have
hope." Rom. xv. 4.

O THOU, who from primeval night
Didst call forth light, "*and there was light,*"
Whose mandate stirr'd the void repose,
And order out of chaos rose.

Once more, Eternal *Logos*, shine
On this dark place with pow'r divine;
Our hearts renew, revive and search,
And guide and purify Thy Church.

"*The volume of Thy Book*" unseal,
And to our souls its love reveal:
Unfold Thy truth, unclose our eyes,
And make us to salvation wise.*

While in this desert world we stray,
Thy word shall guide us on the way;
Our hope, until the race is run,
Our verdict, when the work is done.†

* 2 Tim. iii. 15.   † St. John, xii. 38.

SECOND SUNDAY IN ADVENT. No. 2.

He comes! He comes with pow'r divine;
'Midst awful portents He descends;
The moon and stars refuse to shine;
The earth its solid basement rends.

The waves of ocean swell and roar,
And quailing hearts confess their dread,
The nations fall to rise no more,
And the last trump awakes the dead.

He comes! He comes, behold the sign,
Emblazon'd on the flaming sky;
Lift up your heads, ye saints, and shine,
For lo! redemption draweth nigh.

In thrall we lift our hearts to Thee,
Who erst for our transgression died;
Thy welcome Presence sets us free,
O Saviour Christ — The Crucified!

2*

THIRD SUNDAY IN ADVENT.

THE pilèd clouds compose His seat,
And saints and angels form His train,
The heavens are bow'd beneath His feet,
He comes in state to earth again.

He comes His kingdom to restore ;
He comes t' avenge the martyrs' gore :
He comes to set His saints on high,
And reign in Zion gloriously.

On Olivet His steps alight,
The solid mountain cleaves in twain :
Once more the earth at ev'ning bright,
Rejoices in her King again.*

Come, Jesus, come, Thy saints to bless,
Come as the Lord our Righteousness ;
And by Thy pow'r anew create
'This scene in which we watch and wait.

* See Zech. xiv.

THIRD SUNDAY IN ADVENT. No. 2.

"Let a man so account of us, as of the ministers of Christ, and stewards of the mysteries of God. Moreover, it is required in stewards that a man be found faithful." 1 CORINTH. iv. 1, 2.

PROCLAIM the coming day,
Ye ministers of grace ;
Prepare, prepare the sacred way,
Before Messiah's face :
He comes again,
On earth to reign,
O'er our redeemèd race.

Mark well the boding signs,
Ye prophets of the Lord,
And read His merciful designs,
In judgments when abroad,
Ere flaming fire
Reveal the ire
Of His Incarnate Word.

Be faithful to your trust,
Ye stewards of our God,
And strew the wisdom of the just
On paths by sinners trod ;

That He may own
Before His throne,
The purchase of His blood.

Soon shall the work be done,
Ye watchmen on our towers;
Soon shall the promised prize be won,
By all who count the hours
Of life's short scope,
And wait in hope,
For re-created powers.

FOURTH SUNDAY IN ADVENT.

"The Lord is at hand. Be careful for nothing, but in every thing by prayer and supplication with thanksgiving, let your requests be made known unto God." PHIL. iv. 6.

A VOICE to every land
Proclaims, the way prepare,
The Lord is nigh at hand
To judge the world in righteousness,
And with his great salvation bless
His saints, who watch in prayer.

In praise before His throne,
Let ev'ry knee bow down ;
Let ev'ry want be known ;
With joy lift up your heads on high,
For lo ! redemption draweth nigh
His waiting saints to crown.

To prayer ! to prayer ! the cry
Rings through the earth and air,
The day of God is nigh :
Go forth to meet the Bridegroom King,
And to His blest espousals bring
The sacrifice of prayer.

In faith and patience wait,
The blissful scene to share,
When He shall come in state :
And all whose bridal lamps will burn,
Who care for nought but His return,
Shall be transform'd in prayer.*

* " And it came to pass that as He prayed He was transfigured."
St. Luke, ix. 28.

Then nobler notes of song,
In purer strains shall rise,
His praises to prolong :
Whose blissful reign shall never cease,
Who keeps the heart in perfect peace,
That on His blood relies.

FOURTH SUNDAY IN ADVENT. No. 2.

WAIT, Zion, wait, thy Saviour King
Has now in triumph poised His wing,
And hosts of angels round Him throng,
To line His path and shout His song.

The Great Archangel's trumpet blends
With the resistless voice of God,
'Midst shouting thousands he descends,
To tread the earth that erst He trod.

O make us, in that dreadful day,
On Thee, Incarnate Lord, to stay ;
That, when we hear Thy well-known voice,
We may with fearless hearts rejoice.

Wait, Zion, wait, thy saints who cry
Beneath thy altar-steps shall wake ;
To meet the Lord enthronèd high,
When the eternal day shall break.

CHRISTMAS DAY.

O sweet is the sound that awakes with the
  morn,
The sound of glad tidings, Messiah is born ;
" The only begotten," but now stooping low,
To save us from sin and defend us from woe.

Though friendless, and cradled with beasts of
  the stall,
Still carol'd by angels the Saviour of all ;
" Desire of the nations," and claiming a
  throne,
But scornèd by others, denied by His own.

O lowly-born Saviour, Thy presence we greet,
And pour our oblations of praise at Thy feet ;
O " Son of the Highest," look down from
  above,
And make us forever abide in Thy love.

Sweet, sweet is the chorus we hear in the
    skies,
The anthem when cherub to seraph replies ;
To God in the Highest all glory be given,
And peace upon earth and good will be from
    heaven.

CHRISTMAS DAY. No. 2.

"Behold a virgin shall conceive and be with child, and shall bring forth a Son, and they shall call his name EMMANUEL, which being interpreted is, GOD WITH US." ST. MATTH. i. 23.

ARISE and join th' angelic song,
    First carol'd to the earth,
When glory wrapp'd th' adoring throng,
    That sung the Saviour's birth.

Arise and see that " *Holy Thing*," *
    Though lowly born, divine ;
Arise and hail the Promised King,
    Of David's house and line.†

* St. Luke, i. 35.   † St. Luke, i. 69.

He comes, the Son of God, Most High ;
   A pent-house is His bed ;
Emmanuel! God eternally,
   A suff'rer in our stead.

He comes the slave to disenthral,
   Beyond all price the cost ;
He comes to give his life for all,
   The ransom of the lost.

From land to land, in sacred mirth,
   Let the glad tidings run,
And tell to all who dwell on earth,
   The work of grace is done.

ST. STEPHEN'S DAY.

THE first to close this mortal race,
With lion heart and angel face,
Thy martyr Stephen takes the place ;
Confessing Thee, by Thee confess'd,
     He sinks to rest.

3

First to adore th' ascended Lord,
When, kneeling on the gory sward,
He claimed the promise of Thy word,
And found in Thee a refuge nigh,
       Within the sky.

'Midst stones of deadly aim he falls,
'Midst angry threats for mercy calls,
Till Christ his spirit disenthrals ;
Then, with one cry of anguish deep,
       He falls asleep.

O thou Incarnate Deity,
Roll back the screen that hideth Thee,
That our unclouded eyes may see
The reflex glory of Thy face,
       In this dark place.

In all the storms and straits of life,
When sorrows rise and foes are rife;
Come, Jesus, come, and still the strife ;
And as we yield our fleeting breath,
       Bless us in death.

ST. JOHN THE EVANGELIST.

O God of love, to Thee we raise
Our voices high in songs of praise ;
To bless Thee for the light serene,
That shone on Patmos' desert scene.

We praise Thee for that vision clear,
Which all thy churches list to hear ;
Which all thy waiting saints receive,
The earnest of the earth's reprieve.

Dispel our fears, disperse our night ;
Speed through the earth thy Gospel's flight,
That in the light of Truth we may
Attain the eternal light of day.

Around us when the darkness rolls,
O " Light of Light," illume our souls ;
And guide us to that place above,
Where thine elect abide in love.

THE INNOCENTS' DAY.

In vain the heathen spend their ire
On mourning Judah's infant race ;
Though thousands fall by sword and fire,
Thousands arise to fill their place.

O Lord, bedew'd with martyr's gore
Thy church shall flourish more and more ;
And ev'rywhere Thy people spread,
Baptized in danger for the dead.

O Rachel, for thy children slain,
Be comforted and cease to weep ;
No longer let thy tongue complain,
Safe in their Saviour's arms they sleep.

Convert our hearts, O Lord, to Thee,
And from transgression set us free ;
Then take us to that land of peace,
Where tyrants from their troubling cease.

SUNDAY AFTER CHRISTMAS DAY. No. 1.

" And she shall bring forth a Son, and thou shalt call his name JESUS ; for he shall save his people from their sins."   St. Matth. i. 21.

O JESUS, Thy beloved name
Inspires my heart and lifts my voice,
To tell to list'ning worlds its fame,
And in its saving power rejoice.

Though lowly born, divinely named,
The heir of heaven, to earth assign'd ;
And by the Angel's voice proclaim'd
The only Saviour of mankind.

My tower of strength to which I fly ; *
In time of war my conq'ring arm ;
My covert when the storm is nigh,
My perfect rest when it is calm.

O JESUS, to Thy name I bow,
The earnest of Thy grace and love ;
And with it written on my brow,
Will I approach Thy throne above.†

* Proverbs, xviii. 10.   † Rev. xxii. 4.

.3*

Its fragrance is my vital breath,
The sign and seal of sins forgiven;
My comfort in the hour of death,
My watchword at the gate of heaven.

SUNDAY AFTER CHRISTMAS DAY. No. 2.

" That which hath been is now ; and that which is to be hath already
been ; and God requireth that which is past." ECCLES. iii. 15.

O WHAT a fleeting thing is life,
  No halting time is known ;
The years which came with promise rife,
  With lightning speed are flown.

The things that *were* have glided past,
  We grasp the present *now* ;
But while we think to hold it fast,
  'Tis gone, we know not how.

The promised future, by a pall
  Though hidden from our ken,
Comes quickly, if it come at all,
  And slighted *now* is *then*.

The *Past!* the Past with all its tale
  Of actions and desires;
The past, though in our mem'ry pale,
  Is that which God requires.

Watch! watch the rapid flight of life,
  Its course brooks no delay;
It binds alike our peace and strife,
  To *now*, the present day.

Soon shall the mighty angel stride
  The ocean and its shore:
And swear above its troubled tide,
  " *That Time shall be no more.*"

THE CIRCUMCISION.

O Lord, another measured space,
  Like the neglected last,
Has onward roll'd its ceaseless tide,
  And mingled with the past.

How many years have fled away,
  All unimproved, unblest ;
O let not this as profitless
  Be number'd with the rest !

Thou oft hast spared, O spare us still,
  To run our destined race ;
And cause us, as we grow in years
  Alike to grow in grace.

Imprint the wings of present Time,
  With wisdom in their flight,
And make us with the new-born year,
  New creatures in Thy sight.

THE EPIPHANY.

In eastern skies the mystic Star,
Is onward travelling fast and far ;
And sages track its guiding ray
Across Arabia's desert way.

Or can it be an angel blest,
Clad in some bright and glorious vest,
To lead us where, in lowly shed,`
The kingly Saviour lays his head ?

Our best oblations, Christ, we bring,
And own Thee Prophet, Priest and King ;
Accept our praise and grant our prayer,
And guide and guard us ev'rywhere.

O be our light upon the road,
That leads to glory and to God ;
The bright and morning Star, whose ray
Shines more and more to perfect day.

FIRST SUNDAY AFTER EPIPHANY. No. 1.

"They found him in the midst of the doctors, both hearing them and asking them questions." St. Luke, ii. 46.

O LIVING Saviour, meek and mild,
Who once became a little child,
To teach us by Thy perfect ways,
How we should spend our early days.

O let Thy blest example serve
To guide our footsteps lest we swerve;
While tender, bend our wills to Thee,
And keep us from pollution free.

Distil Thy doctrine like the dew,
Our minds enlarge, our hearts renew,
That we may sit beneath Thy feet,
And worship at Thy mercy seat.

O Saviour, still vouchsafe to bless
Thy children who around Thee press;
Though erring oft, Thy wrath restrain,
And fold us in Thy arms again.

FIRST SUNDAY AFTER EPIPHANY. No. 2.

THE Day-star in our hearts at last,
  Has risen in lustre bright ;
And on the darken'd world has cast
  Its sure and guiding light.

With joy we hail the dawning day,
  And our first offerings bring ;
To Thee the willing tribute pay,
  Our Prophet, Priest and King.

It is not gold from Ophir's mine,
  Nor spice from eastern grove ;
Our hearts we offer at Thy shrine,
  The sacrifice of love.

We offer up at Thy behest,
  Ourselves transform'd by Thee,
Our bodies by Thy Spirit blest,
  Our souls by Truth made free.*

* Rom. xii. 1, 2.

We come to yield this service, Lord,
   And, with our utmost skill,
To learn the doctrines of Thy word,
   And do Thy blessed will.

SECOND SUNDAY AFTER THE EPIPHANY.

" And both Jesus was called and his disciples to the marriage."
St. John, ii. 2.

THE bridal lamps shone bright
In Cana's favor'd hall ;
For Thou, O Christ, that night
Didst bless the festival.
In ev'ry scene of mirth,
In ev'ry time of fear,
At Burial, Bridal, Birth,
'Tis good to have Thee near.

To mark in prosp'rous day
Thy ready hand to save ;
To feel Thy beamy ray
When sinking to the grave.

Come, Lord, in all our straits,
And by Thy word divine,
Turn, as in Cana's gates,
Our water into wine.

Turn weakness into power,
Turn darkness into light ;
And gild each sadden'd hour,
And give us songs at night.
Our fightings and our fears
Exchange for peace and love,
And give us, for our tears,
Eternal joys above.

THIRD SUNDAY AFTER EPIPHANY.
" Lord, I have loved the habitation of thy house."　PSALM XXVI. 8.

WE love the place, O Lord,
Wherein Thine honor dwells ;
The joy of Thy abode
All other joy excels.

We love the House of prayer,
Wherein Thy servants meet ;
For Thou, O Lord, art there,
Thy chosen ones to greet.

4

We love the sacred Font
Wherein the Holy Dove
Pours out, as He is wont,
The effluence from above.

We love our Father's board,
Its altar steps are dear ;
For there is faith adored,
We find Thy Presence near.

We love Thy saints who come
Thy mercy to proclaim,
To call the wand'rers home,
And magnify Thy name.

Our first and latest love
To Zion shall be given —
The House of God above,
On earth the Gate of Heav'n.

FOURTH SUNDAY AFTER EPIPHANY.

" Be not conformed to this world." Rom. xii. 2.

O LORD, before Thy gracious throne
We bow the suppliant knee,
Well pleased our bodies (not our own)
To offer up to Thee.

The world appears, on ev'ry side,
With glitt'ring pomp to blind ;
Its gains, its pleasures, and its pride,
Our souls in fetters bind.

We meet the world in ev'ry sound,
That drowns Thy gracious voice —
In all the objects that surround
And misdirect our choice.

We meet it in the crowded mart,
We meet it when alone ;
It dwells within our secret heart,
And there erects its throne.

O Lord, transform us by Thy grace,
  Renew us from above ;
And let no idol find a place
  To rival Thee in love.

FIFTH SUNDAY AFTER EPIPHANY.

With thankful hearts to God, our King,
The tribute of our praise we bring ;
O let it to Thy throne arise
As incense from the sacrifice.

In all the varied scenes of life,
In helpless age, in manhood's strife,
In ev'ry place, in ev'ry hour,
Our steps are guarded by Thy power.

When sickness bows the aching head,
Thy hand shall easy make our bed ;
And when with fears of sin opprest,
Thy " *still small voice* " shall give us rest.

·O let Thy word .within us dwell,
Our hearts inspire, our voices swell,
In psalms and hymns and sacred songs,
The glory that to God belongs.

In midnight gloom, or cloudless day,
On God alone our trust we stay ;
In fetters bound, or soaring free,
Our first, last thanks shall be to Thee.

SIXTH SUNDAY AFTER EPIPHANY.

"O wretched man that I am ! who shall deliver me from the body of this death ? I thank God, through Jesus Christ our Lord." ROMANS, vii. 24, 25.

BESET with sin, oppress'd with fear,
    To Jesus we repair ;
Be Thou our refuge ever near,
    And save us from despair.

The high resolve we make in vain,
    For treason lurks within ;
We rise to good, but fall again
    Beneath the law of sin.

4*

The thoughts of the redeemless past
  Pervade each present hour,
And on awaken'd mem'ry cast
  Their stern and awful power.

Inconstant, weak, to Thee we fly,
  On Thee for succor call;
O guide us safely with Thine eye,
  And raise us when we fall.

And for Thy mercy's sake we pray
  Repentance for the past;
That, aided by Thy grace, we may
  Be conquerors at last.

SUNDAY CALLED SEPTUAGESIMA.

"And he said, Let there be light; and there was light." Gen. i. 3.

O source divine of life and light,
Beneath whose wing primeval night
    Became a radiant dawn;
Whose word dispell'd the ebon shade,
That on the formless void was laid,
    Before the earth was born.

Come with Thy brooding power once more,
And let Thy Word the earth restore
    To righteousness again ;
Like to a burning lamp go forth
From Judah to the utmost north,
    From Zion to the main.

O holy Dove, who on the head
Of Jesus Christ Thy radiance shed,
    In Jordan's limpid wave ;
Who by the tongues of plastic flame,
Gave power in His prevailing name,
    The sinful world to save ;

Again Thy presence we implore ;
Come as Thou wilt, and hover o'er
    The chosen of the earth ;
Let Thy good Spirit now impart,
New health and gladness to the heart,
    And bless our Second Birth.

SUNDAY CALLED SEXAGESIMA.

With sadden'd hearts the joys we scan,
Before on Eden fell the ban
   Of treason and its woes ;
Which changed the flow'ry vale of earth
Into a desert land and dearth,
   And peopled it with foes.

No more the garden blooms serene ;
No more the face of God is seen
   Within its peaceful bowers ;
Sin upon all its blight has shed,
And Death with darkness overspread
   Its bright and blissful hours.

One fatal lure with man prevail'd,
One fatal deed the curse entail'd,
   " And *dying thou shalt die ;* " *
And we must yield, but, in our stead,
The curse has fallen on Jesus' head,
   And brought redemption nigh.

    * Gen. ii. 17. Marginal reading.

Redeem'd and saved by love divine,
Make us, O Christ, forever Thine,
   To live by faith in Thee ;
And wait in patience till the time,
When earth shall bloom as in the prime,
   From sin and sorrow free.

SUNDAY CALLED QUINQUAGESIMA.

"O Lord, thou has taught us that all our doings without charity are
nothing worth." COLLECT.

It naught avails that we proclaim
With angel tongue, God's matchless fame ;
In vain the martyr's stake we share,
If thou, sweet Love, art absent there.

The prophet's ken, the preacher's fire,
And Faith and Hope alike expire ;
All other graces fade and die,
But love shall live eternally.

For " *God is love*," and love alone
Shall share the glory of His throne —
The nearest to behold His face,
The highest to receive his grace.

The love, O Son of God most High,
That brought Thee here to bleed and die,
Constrains our love to all distrest,
And blessing others makes us blest.

O Christ, O Love without compare,
In Thy rich mercies let us share ;
That by Thy great Example, we
May dwell in love eternally.

SUNDAY CALLED QUINQUAGESIMA.   No. 2.

"I do set my bow in the cloud," &c.   GEN. ix. 13.

WHEN threat'ning clouds deform the skies,
And danger on the tempest flies,
" *The Bow is set ;* " no more alarm ;
God speaks the word, and it is calm.

When Sin, with death and all its woes,
Breaks wildly in on our repose,
" *The Bow is set*," and through our tears
The Sun of Righteousness appears.

When toss'd with sickness through the night,
His grace can make affliction light ;
" *The Bow is set*," and at the dawn,
Its radiant hues shall bless the morn.

Of goods and friends on earth bereft,
Still hope, sweet hope of heaven is left ;
" *The Bow is set ;* " we kiss the rod,
And find our wealth and friends in God.

When sinking to the last repose,
The grave on earthly hopes shall close,
" *The Bow is set ;* " our weary march
Is stay'd beneath its glorious arch.

Aye, glorious when the dead shall wake,
And the eternal day shall break,
With seven-fold light, to shine upon
The Emerald Bow around the throne.*

* Isaiah, xxx. 26.   Rev. iv. 3.

FIRST DAY OF LENT, COMMONLY CALLED ASH WEDNESDAY.

"Repent ye, for the kingdom of heaven is at hand." St. Matth. iii. 2.

Mourn, Zion, mourn thy ways perverse,
   Let ev'ry knee be bent;
Let ev'ry tongue the cry rehearse
   To every ear, *Repent!*

Then be this season ev'rywhere
   In deep contrition spent;
And grant Thy mercy to the prayer
   Of all who now *repent.*

O make our eyes gush out with tears,
   For all Thy gifts mispent;
And far remove the harrowing fears
   Of failing to *repent.*

O Saviour-Prince, exalted high,
   Thy threaten'd wrath relent;
Remission give, and lest we die,
   Give wisdom to *repent.**

* Acts, v. 31.

ASH WEDNESDAY. No. 2.

For in thy sight shall no man living be justified." PSALM cxliii. 2.

THOU, Lord, alone art pure,
And none are good, save Thee ;
None can Thy searching eye endure,
None from Thy sentence flee.
Our deeds, by mortals scann'd,
Though passing good they seem,
When weighed by Thy impartial hand,
" Fly up and kick the beam."

Our pleasure and our gain,
When brought beneath Thine eye,
Are marr'd and spotted with a stain
Dark as the Tyrian dye.
In thoughts of God within,
In solemn acts of prayer,
In all our holy things we sin,
And condemnation share.

5 .

To Thee alone we fly,
On Thee we cast our care ;
O Saviour, Thou, when throned on high,
Shalt answer for us there.*
With robes made white in blood,
From sin and death set free ;
Our souls, emerging from the flood,
Shall stand complete in Thee.†

ASH WEDNESDAY.   No. 3.

THE   LAST   DAY.

THE day will come ! a day of gloom,
Of sorrow and dismay ;
The day will come, the day of doom,
Thy day, O Christ ; — " THAT *day !* "
The heavens shall bow beneath Thy feet,
And earth shall melt with fervent heat.

* Psalm xxxviii. 15.   † Colos. ii. 10.

When Thy hot thunderbolts are hurl'd,
And lightnings flash with ire,
And desolation on the world
Bursts in a flood of fire ;
Then all that know not *Thee* shall die,
And perish everlastingly.

Though all creation feel the shock,
There shall no harm nor loss
Befall that blood-bought little flock,
Who glory in the cross ;
Who guided by Thy staff and rod,
Depart in peace to meet their God.

O take us, then, Almighty King,
And keep us from the blast,
Beneath the shadow of Thy wing,
Until the storm be past ;
Till heaven and earth shall newly rise
In purer form, 'neath calmer skies.

ASH WEDNESDAY. No. 4.

" For thou writest bitter things against me, and makest me to possess the iniquities of my youth." Job, xiii. 26.

WHEN sad and dismay'd my past life I survey,
And think on the sins which no numbers can
    tell,
I tremble with fear, while I venture to pray,
To rescue my soul from the nethermost hell.

When the sins of my youth stand out in array,
I am made my forgotten transgressions to
    guage ;
They rush on the mind like the scene of a day,
And leave me condemn'd to the wrath of an
    age.

I am guilty and lost, but to Thee I repair,
In the name of the Lord, the sinner's retreat ;
Have pity, have pity, nor cast out my prayer,
Nor leave mé to die in despair at Thy feet.

On my soul let the stream of Thy mercy be
    pour'd,
And all my transgressions forever efface,
To serve Thee, my Saviour, reclaim'd and
    restor'd,
Redeem'd by Thy blood, and renew'd by Thy
    grace.

FIRST SUNDAY IN LENT. No. 1.

"Then was Jesus led up of the Spirit to be tempted of the devil."
ST. MATTH. iv. 1.

The Foe! the foe is on the path,
  -Gird up your loins and fly;
Brief is the time, but great the wrath; *
  Escape him or ye die.

Where'er our careless footsteps stray,
  In each unguarded hour,
Like lion greedy for his prey,
  He watches to devour.

* Rev. xii. 12.

5*

In ev'ry scene we meet the foe ;
　In Mammon's spangled vest ;
And round us his enchantments glow,
　In Pleasure loosely drest.

High plumed in mad Ambition's flight ;
　In Vanity's attire ;
Or as an angel robed in light,
　To mock Devotion's fire.*

Triumphant Lord, before whose frown
　The Tempter must retreat,
Now aid us, and at last beat down
　The Foe beneath out feet.†

FIRST SUNDAY IN LENT. No. 2.

" Jehovah Jireh."　Gen. xxii. 14.
" The Lord will provide."　Marginal Reading."

To Thee, O Lord, I make my prayer,
On Thee alone I cast my care,
　Whatever ills betide ;

* 2 Cor. x. 14.　　　　　　† Litany.

Whatever be the stern decree,
I know that " all things come of Thee,"*
    To help and to provide.

In time of need, in scenes of strife,
When wants press hard, and foes are rife,
    Still Thou art by my side :
To raise up friends to be my stay,
Whose acts of kindness seem to say,
    Thy Saviour will provide.

When Satan tempts my heart to stray,
And casts allurements in my way,
    To turn my steps aside ;
Then, with the panoply complete,
In which the subtle foe to meet,
    The Lord God will provide.

When sin-oppress'd, I sink with grief,
And nought of earth can bring relief,
    In Thee I still confide ;
O, Jesus, Thou, and Thou alone,
Shalt answer for me at the Throne,
    And safety shalt provide.

* 1 Chron. xxix. 14.

In danger on the flood and field,
Thou art, O Lord, my Sun and Shield,
    My guardian and my guide :
And as in days already past,
I'll grasp Thy promise to the last,
    " Jehovah will provide."

Soon will the strife of earth be o'er,
And we shall meet (to part no more,)
    The Bridegroom and the Bride :
Then in the wedding garment drest,
All that I need to make me blest,
    My Saviour will provide.

SECOND SUNDAY IN LENT.

" Come unto me all ye that labour and are heavy laden, and I will give
you rest." St. Matth. xi. 28.

How sweet in troubled life,
  When careworn and distrest,
To hear a voice above the strife —
  Come, weary soul, and rest.

Come, with Thy aching heart ;
Come, with thy streaming eye ;
Come, weak and weary as thou art—
None come to me and die.

The face of Jesus seek ;
On Him thy burden roll ;
His saving grace supports the weak ;
He makes the wounded whole.
He bids the lab'rer cease ;
He sets the captive free ;
He brings the contrite sinner peace ;
And rest remains for thee.

They who His aid invoke,
Can never be cast down ;
And they, who take His easy yoke,
Shall wear His glorious crown.
Jesus, Thy mercy send,
Absolve and set us free ;
And all our new-born powers shall bend
To *work* and *rest* in Thee.

THIRD SUNDAY IN LENT.

"Awake, thou that sleepest, and arise from the dead, and Christ shall give thee light." EPH. v. 14.

O SLUMBERING soul, awake!
The Spirit loudly calls;
At once arise renew'd, and break
The chain thy soul enthrals.

O son of death, arise!
The Saviour bids thee live;
Press onward for the glorious prize,
The prize that Christ shall give.

Fold not thine arms to sleep,
And ask no more delay;
Awake, and with contrition deep,
Arise and watch and pray.

O weary soul, awake!
Soon on this dreary night
An everlasting day shall break,
"*And Christ shall give thee light.*"

FOURTH SUNDAY IN LENT.

With painèd heart and streaming eye,
Lord, to Thy mercy seat we fly ;
O let us Thy compassion share,
And save our souls from dark despair.

Too long, O Lord, our steps have swerv'd,
Too long Thy threatened wrath deserv'd ;
Still pity Thou our sad estate,
Nor let repentance come too late.

Send us repentance from above,
And with it send Thy pardoning love ;
And let the blood which Jesus spilt,
Remove our shame, atone our guilt.

Awake and by Thy Spirit seal'd,
Our new-born souls to Thee we yield ;
Thy grace shall make the evening light,
And furnish songs throughout the night.

And when the work of grace is done,
And sin is spoil'd, and heav'n is won,
Within that pure and safe retreat,
Our crowns shall lie beneath Thy feet.

FIFTH SUNDAY IN LENT.

SWEET, in the times of sore distress,
  Thy words, O Saviour, prove ;
And sweet, when fears our souls oppress,
  The mem'ry of Thy love.

How can we grieve, when Thou art nigh
  To calm the troubled breast ?
How can we fear, when we may fly
  To Thee for peace and rest ?

O Jesus, lover of our souls,
  Thy grace to us extend ;
And when the tide of sorrow rolls,
  Our fainting souls defend.

And when the mortal eye and ear
  To sights and sounds are seal'd,
Then open to our vision dear
  The glory unreveal'd.

SUNDAY NEXT BEFORE EASTER.

HOSANNA! let your voices ring,
He comes, the long predicted King,
  With palm-leaves strew the ground :
Meekly he comes to Zion's gate,
Without the retinue of state,
  But with salvation crown'd.
                    Hosanna !

Hosanna ! though in lowly mien,
The Prince of Peace is dimly seen,
  He comes on mission high ;
Applauding crowds confess His name,
A voice from Heaven attests His fame,
  In audible reply.
                    Hosanna !

Hosanna ! though a sadden'd song,
In tones subdued, we still prolong,
  With all Thy chosen train ;
O may we, with this blessed few,
In accents ever sweet and new,
  Revive the grateful strain.
                    Hosanna !

6

MONDAY BEFORE EASTER.

PATIENCE.

It is a world of woes,
But we will not complain ;
Its sorrows and its throes
Are never sent in vain.

The clouds obscure the sky,
We know that Thou art there ;
Our loving Lord on high,
On whom to cast our care.

When 'midst severest ill,
The tide of sorrow rolls,
O let thy patience still
In peace possess our souls.

Thy temper, meek and pure,
With all our feelings blend,
And teach us to endure,
And save us in the end.

O Lord, with foes o'erprest,
With sorrows overborne,
With mockery distrest,
With thorns and scourges torn;

Left on the cross to die,
Exposed, and bound, and nail'd,
Though forced with pain to cry,
Thy patience never fail'd.

Whatever be Thy will,
Or be it grief or pain,
Our hearts shall not rebel,
Our tongues shall not complain.

Turn not Thy face away,
Thou, uncomplaining One,
While we submissive pray,
O Lord, Thy will be done.

TUESDAY BEFORE EASTER.

HUMILITY.

"And being found in fashion as a man, He humbled Himself, and became obedient unto death, even the death of the cross." PHIL. ii. 7.

'T was stooping low, immortal King,
   To clothe in mortal guise ;
And as a man, for man, to bring
   Salvation from the skies.

'T was lowlier still, to lay aside
   The pomp and power of God,
And in a servant's form to bide
   The cruel smiter's rod.

Prostrate before Thy glorious throne,
   Our vileness we confess ;
And rest our hope in Thee alone,
   The Lord our Righteousness.

Our greatest gain we count but loss,
   And all the world beside,
Our only glory is the Cross,
   Our boast — THE CRUCIFIED.

WEDNESDAY BEFORE EASTER.

SELF-DENIAL.

"Then said Jesus unto his disciples, if any man will come after me, let him deny himself, and take up his cross and follow me." St. Matth. xvi. 24.

To follow Thee! and must we tread
The path Thy martyr'd saints have trod,
And must we bleed as Thou hast bled,
And strew with woes our way to God?

To follow Thee! and must we bear
The Cross Thy failing heart o'erprest,
And with relentless purpose tear
The dearest objects from our breast?

To follow Thee! and must we drink
The bitter cup that Thou didst drain,
Nor from the fiery baptism shrink,
That bathed Thy soul in unknown pain?

O give us patience to endure,
O give us faith to overcome;
And let Thy saving strength secure
Thy promises beyond the tomb.

6*

And teach us, when we pause with fear,
Or when our spirits shrink with pain,
That they who suffer with Thee here,
With Thee in endless bliss shall reign.

THURSDAY BEFORE EASTER.

FORGIVENESS.

" Father, forgive them, for they know not what they do." St. Luke,
xxiii. 34.

Our sins, O Saviour Christ, forgive,
And let redeemèd sinners live ;
Deserving wrath, to Thee we fly,
And on Thy saving grace rely.

Unnumber'd sins the mem'ry crowd,
And all our hopes of mercy shroud ;
But through the gloom we look to Thee,
And make Thy dying prayer our plea.

Dear is that cry amidst Thy woes,
The pray'r for pardon to Thy foes ;
For when we sin, it still is true,
We know not all the wrong we do.

We do not know the open shame,
We cast upon *Immanuel's name*,
We do not know that we deny
The Saviour, and His wrath defy.

O holy Victim, let us share
The merit of that dying prayer;
Once more repeat its pleading tone,
As on the Cross, now on the throne.

GOOD FRIDAY. No. 1.

THE whole creation groans with pain,
    And darkness shrouds the land;
The temple vail is rent in twain,
    Untouch'd by mortal hand.

The mountains to their basement reel,
    As though convulsed with dread;
The op'ning graves their depths reveal,
    And yield their sainted dead.

'T is finishèd! the Saviour cries,
   And bows His bleeding head;
'T is finishèd! the world replies,
   He suffers in our stead.

O spotless Lamb, our sins remove;
   So from the curse set free,
We may, constrainèd by Thy love,
   Live evermore to Thee.

GOOD FRIDAY. No. 2.

AND who is He, with visage marr'd,
   And raiment stained with gore,
With thorns and scourges torn and scarr'd,
   And still to suffer more?

Ah! whence that deep and painèd cry,
   That rends the darken'd skies?
'T is the last wail of agony,
   Christ bows his head and dies.

Alone, Thou hast the Cross endured,
  Alone the wine-press trod ;
Alone, our peace Thou hast secured,
  Our Saviour and our God.

Our sins have drawn Thy precious blood,
  And cover'd Thee with shame :
O cleanse us with its healing blood,
  And save our souls from blame.

GOOD FRIDAY. No. 3.

FROM prison to the judgment led,
Mock'd, spat upon, and buffeted,
By foes accused, by friends denied,
Convicted, scourg'd, and crucified,
  None came to His relief ;
    Suspended high,
    And left to cry,
With unavailing grief.

His quiv'ring limbs distraught with pain,
His parchèd lips of thirst complain ;
By man reviled, by God condemn'd,
Oppress'd, forsaken, overwhelmed
　　In body and in mind,
　　　　And left alone,
　　　　With blood t' atone
　For guilt of all mankind.

The riven rocks and darken'd sun,
Proclaim to all the work is done ;
The world is saved which sin defiled,
" And God with sinners reconciled,"
　　The vail is rent in twain,
　　　　Gentile and Jew,
　　　　Are born anew,
　" *The enmity is slain.*"

EASTER EVEN.

"Now in the place where He was crucified, there was a garden; and in the garden a new sepulchre." St. John, xix. 41.

TREAD softly on that bed of flow'rs
　　Which in the garden bloom;
For hidden 'midst its fairy bowers,
　　Is oftentimes a tomb.

In childhood's day, with lightsome step,
　　We skip from scene to scene;
And heed not things that intercept
　　The path that lies between.

And then in manhood's strength and strife,
　　For lengthen'd days we crave;
And heed not in the midst of life,
　　We stand upon the grave.

O may we be prepared by grace;
　　And when the hour shall come,
The Crucified be near the place,
　　Where we shall make our tomb.

EASTER DAY. No. 1.

In triumph clap your hands,
And swell the joyful lay,
And tell to distant lands
That Christ is rais'd to-day.
His name adore
In sweetest strains,
Messiah reigns,
And dies no more.

Angels the seal have cleft,
And roll'd away the stone.
The grave of tenant reft,
Proclaims salvation won.
The strife is o'er,
With Hell and Death ;
His vital breath
Shall cease no more.

Again our hearts rejoice,
And all our troubles cease ;
Again His gentle voice
We hear, in tones of peace.
Messiah reigns
For evermore ;
In highest strains,
His name adore.

EASTER DAY. No. 2.

" For ye are dead, and your life is hid with Christ in God : When
Christ who is our life shall appear, then shall ye also appear with him in
glory." COLOS. iii. 3, 4.

O GOD of Glory and of Grace,
Look down on our apostate race ;
And cause the rays of light divine
On our benighted state to shine.

Lift up our thoughts to things above,
And fill our hearts with light and love ;
Our souls re-clothe and elevate,
And all their powers anew create.

7

Releas'd from sin, reliev'd from pain,
The sons of God shall shout again ;
And with the morning stars shall sing
The song of joy to Christ our King.

O hasten, Lord, the glorious day,
When heav'n and earth shall flee away ;
When all Thy waiting saints are seal'd,
And all their hidden life reveal'd.

When, gladden'd by Thy welcome voice,
The dead and living shall rejoice ;
In one long, loud, harmonious strain,
" The Christ appears on earth again " !

EASTER DAY. No. 3.

WELL pleas'd, O Lord, we linger, where
  Bright angel-forms are seen ;
And angel-voices fill the air,
  With melody serene.

Where angel-guards the tomb defend,
  In which the Saviour lay;
And angel-guides His faithful friend
  To Jesus point the way.

We feel Thy gracious Spirit near,
  Thy words our hearts rejoice;
And in Thy promises we hear
  Thy recognizing voice.

In all our doubts, in all our fears,
  Our fainting souls befriend;
Rabboni, Master, dry our tears,
  And speedy succor send.

EASTER DAY. No. 4.

"He is not here, but is risen." St. Luke, xxiv. 6.

Awake, awake, the dawning ray
Has shed its glories on the day;
With gladden'd hearts arise, and sing
The matin anthem to our King.

By man betray'd, alone He trode
" *The wine-press of the wrath of God ;* " *
Alone He wrought the world to save,
And went unpitied to the grave.

Awake! awake! no more the gloom
Hangs o'er the Saviour's guarded tomb ;
" *He is not here, but risen* " on high,
From death reviv'd, no more to die.†

Hail, Jesus! once by man ignor'd,
By saints and angels now ador'd ;
Once marr'd and weak, now cloth'd in might ;
Once crown'd with thorns, now crown'd with
            light.

Wake, tenants of the dust, and sing,
Your buried Saviour now is King ;
Arise! and with the angels cry,
" O, grave, where is thy victory " !

* Isaiah, lxiii. 3.   Revel. xix. 15.   † Romans, vi. 9.

EASTER DAY. No. 5.

My heart is fix'd on things above,
Where Jesus sits enthron'd in love;
On scenes beyond our mortal ken,
Where Jesus pleads for sinful men.

Before the throne, where odors rise
Of His accepted sacrifice;
Odors commingl'd with the plaints
Of suff'ring and rejoicing saints.

When arms are weak, and eyes are dim,
My heart with gladness springs to Him,
Who wrought for me His Father's will,
And lives my Intercessor still.

My thronèd Priest, my mitred King,
To Thee my heart's affections cling;
And joy and peace in concord meet
Before Thy gracious mercy-seat.

7*

My Saviour, crucified and slain,
Once dead, now rais'd to life again;
Stretch forth Thy mighty arm, and save
My soul in triumph from the grave.

Then raise me up to places high,
To dwell with Thee eternally;
Where praise shall fill my charmèd breath,
With no more sin and no more death.

EASTER MONDAY.

"Because he hath appointed a day, in the which he will judge the world in righteousness by that man whom he hath ordained; whereof he hath given assurance unto all men, in that he hath raised him from the dead." ACTS, xvii. 31.

EXALTED Lord, we wait the hour,
With mingl'd thoughts of hope and dread,
When Thou shalt come, in pomp and pow'r,
To judge the living and the dead;

When all, to earth's remotest bound,
The trumpet and the voice shall hear;
And all, responsive to the sound,
Before the throne of Christ appear;

When thoughts of sin and deeds of night,
Although from mortal eye conceal'd,
Shall, by Omniscience brought to light,
To men and angels be reveal'd.

And who, in that decisive day,
Shall answer for us at Thy throne?
Who, turn Thy burning wrath away,
And for our guilty souls atone?

O Jesus, Lord of pow'r and might,
Cleanse us from sin, and make us meet
To mingle with Thy saints in light,
And stand before Thy judgment-seat.

EASTER TUESDAY.

"Because I live, ye shall live also." St. John, xiv. 19.

AND can it be, exalted King,
That underneath Thy downy wing,
 Shall be our 'biding place ;
That when Thou art in glory dight,
With angels we shall " walk in white,"
 And see Thee face to face ?

And can it be our souls shall rest,
Among the spirits pure and blest,
 That gather round Thy throne ;
Unpain'd by grief, unstain'd by sin,
To join th' enraptur'd Seraphim,
 And make their song our own ?

We know not in what glory drest,
We then shall stand among the blest,
 With Him who came to save ;

" *But this we know*," that we shall wake,
Like Him whose glorious word shall break
 The silence of the grave.*

We know that when this house of clay
Shall from our spirits pass away,
 A nobler one shall rise ;
With no decay and no defect,
But, like its mighty Architect,
 Eternal in the skies.†

FIRST SUNDAY AFTER EASTER.

" Jesus stood in the midst, and said unto them, Peace be unto you."
JOHN, xx. 19.

WHEN to Thy presence, Lord, we near,
 Our sorrows quickly cease ;
And when Thy gentle voice we hear,
 It speaks in tones of peace.

* 1 John, iii. 2.   † 2 Cor. v. 1.

Peace in the Church; in that blest place,
  Where saints are wont to meet;
Peace, faithful souls! for there My face,
  My chosen ones shall greet.

Peace at the Board which I provide
  In Zion's lov'd retreat;
Peace, festive souls! where I preside,
  The spikenard yields its sweet.*

Peace to the man who sinks distress'd,
  When sin is pressing sore;
Peace, wounded soul! with pardon blest,
  Go forth and sin no more.

Peace to the house where mourners live
  In sickness and in pain;
Peace, troubl'd souls! for I will give
  The balm of health again.

Peace at the grave, where sweetly sleep
  The saints from trial free;
Peace, mourning souls! no longer weep
  For those who die in Me.

* Song of Solomon, i. 12.

And when, at last, O gracious Lord,
  From earth we have release ;
Once more, encourag'd by Thy word,
  " Let us depart in peace."

———

SECOND SUNDAY AFTER EASTER.

LIKE erring sheep we go astray,
Far from Thy pure and perfect way ;
And heedless of Thy warning voice,
Take paths of danger for our choice.

O Thou, who for Thy flock hast fled,
Make us to go as we are led ;
Make us to heed Thy gentle voice,
And in Thy guidance to rejoice.

Let us parental favor share,
And guard us with a shepherd's care ;
Watch o'er our paths, our wants provide,
And fold us safe at eventide.

And when upon our path, at last,
The shadows of the grave are cast;
Thy rod and staff support us still,
And lead us to Thy holy hill.

THIRD SUNDAY AFTER EASTER.

"And ye shall be sorrowful, but your sorrow shall be turned into joy.'
St. John, xvi. 20.

Dark are the clouds that o'er me roll,
　Charg'd with avenging ire;
And sin within my burden'd soul,
　Is like a burning fire.

Through all the hours of day or night,
　My heart is fill'd with grief;
In vain I look around for light,
　In vain I seek relief.

In vain for friendly help I crave,
    In vain for pity cry ;
No arm is stretchèd out to save,
    No comforter is nigh.

But when all earthly help is stay'd,
    And earthly friendships fail ;
O Lord, Thy grace shall bring me aid,
    And mercy shall prevail.

As with the golden rays of morn,
    Thy saving health display ;
And all my grief shall soon be gone,
    The clouds shall pass away.

My countless sins to Thee I bring,
    O, " *nail them to the tree,*"*
And with recover'd health, I 'll sing
    The truth has made me free.†

* Colos. ii. 14.   † St. John, viii. 32.

8

FOURTH SUNDAY AFTER EASTER.

FATHER of lights, for good we seek in vain,
In carnal pleasure and in worldly gain ;
All good and perfect gifts from Thee proceed,
Our Guide and Comforter in time of need.

Make us to feel that Thou art good supreme,
And on our path let Thy glad radiance
      beam ;
And with Thy counsel, guide our eyes to see
The unmix'd happiness that flows from Thee.

'T is good, within Thy temple, to prolong
The contrite pray'r, or swell th' enraptur'd
      song ;
'T is good Thy Spirit's *" still small voice "* to
      hear,
And good to feel Thy veilèd presence near.

O Light of Light, in whom we live and move,
Illume our steps with undiminish'd love ;
And at the close, O let the unclouded ray
Shed on our souls its everlasting day.

FIFTH SUNDAY AFTER EASTER.

DEVOTION.

"Hitherto ye have asked nothing in my name; ask and ye shall receive, that your joy may be full." St. John, xvi. 24.*

SAVIOUR of all, in prayer to Thee,
Before Thy throne I bend my knee;
In mercy hear me while I claim
The promise in Thy precious name.

I ask not earth's abundant cheer,
Nor wish in splendor to appear;
All I desire is for my soul,
Thy pard'ning love to make me whole.

'T is much to ask; my sins outrun
The daily marchings of the sun;
But love, exhaustless as his ray,
Can blot them as a cloud away.

'T is much to ask; my heart is weak,
And falters when for aid I seek;
But Thou shalt inward strength supply,
And pray the Father lest I die.

* Gospel for the day.

Teach me to pray, O Uncreate !
Thou all-prevailing Advocate ;
Confirm and crown th' unfailing plea,
" Thy precious blood was shed for me."

O fill my heart with love Divine,
And make my joy resemble Thine ;
Fulness of joy which angels share,
When sinners name Thy name in pray'r.

THE ASCENSION DAY. No. 1.

"Lift up your heads, O ye gates, and be ye lift up, ye everlasting
doors, and the King of Glory shall come in."   PSALM xxiv. 7.

LET heav'n rejoice and earth be glad,
And men and angels join the strain ;
On ether borne, in glory clad,
The absent King returns again.

Ten thousand thousand swell the throng,
To hail with joy the glorious sight ;
Thousands of thousands chant the song
Of welcome, to the realms of light.

Lo! he ascends in mortal guise,
The Lord of heav'n to earth allied ;
He takes the manhood to the skies,
To plead the cause for which he died.

The Son of man, by man disown'd,
Less cared for than the meanest things ; *
Now girt with pow'r, in glory thron'd,
The Lord of Lords, and King of Kings.

O Lamb of God, exalted high,
Extend to us Thy grace and love
To comfort us ; and when we die,
Receive us to Thy joy above.

* Matth. viii. 20.

8*

THE ASCENSION DAY. No. 2.

"He was received up into heaven, and sat on the right hand of God."
ST. MARK, xvi. 19.

UPBORNE through fields of amber light,
The clouds have veil'd Him from our sight;
The heav'ns have flung their portals wide,
And Jesus Christ is glorified.

O Zion, lift thy voice, and sing
The triumph of Thy martyr'd King;
In concord join the welcome hymn,
Of the enraptured Seraphim.

"Worthy the Lamb!" the chorus swell,
Worthy the Lamb in God to dwell;
Worthy the Lamb for sinners slain,
Reviv'd and rais'd to heav'n again.

Exalted Lord, from Thy high throne
Look down with favor on Thine own;
And make us, by Thy Spirit, meet
To live and worship at Thy feet.

THE ASCENSION DAY. No. 3.

"And it came to pass, while He blessed them, He was parted from them, and carried up into heaven." St. Luke, xxiv. 51.

O LET us follow to the scene,
　By faith, though not by sight,
Where last on earth our Lord was seen,
　From whence He took His flight.

Calm, with parental love, He stands
　In majesty erect;
And blesses with uplifted hands
　The few of God's elect.

Then volant with the pow'r supreme,
　He treads the fields of light;
The lambent clouds with glory beam,
　And hide Him from the sight.

But faith, more piercing than the eye,
　Delights to trace His feet;
And on the throne of God most high,
　The Son of Man to greet.

THE SUNDAY AFTER ASCENSION.

In Bethany, His lone retreat,
He shakes the dust from off His feet;
And on the wings of wavy light
Ascends beyond the mortal sight.

Ten thousand saints around him throng,
Ten thousand thousand swell the song;
From world to world is heard the strain,
" *Worthy the Lamb that once was slain.*"

No eye can count, no tongue express,
The mighty hosts that round him press;
And trophies of salvation bring,
To welcome their returning King.

Lift up our hearts, O gracious Lord,
To Thy eternal, blest abode;
Where Thy redeem'd in glory meet,
And cast their crowns beneath Thy feet.

O touch our lips, our hearts inspire,
To join the crown'd and white-robed choir ;
And by Thy grace, our souls prepare,
Their everlasting bliss to share.

WHITSUNDAY.   No. 1.

WITHIN thy gates, on Thee, O Lord,
  Our fainting souls rely ;
And wait, obedient to Thy word,
  The promise from on high.

We wait Thy Spirit's fiery tide,
  Our hearts to cleanse and search ;
We wait the Comforter, to guide
  Thy dearly cherish'd Church.

Once more upon this darken'd place,
  Arise, O Lord, and shine ;
Once more upon an orphan'd race,
  Pour down Thy grace divine.

Come, holy and mysterious fire,
  " Bright effluence " from above ;
Our tongues inflame, our hearts inspire,
  With all-constraining love.

WHITSUNDAY. No. 2.

WE meet within Thy temple gate,
  Thy sacred will to search ;
And in Thy courts to celebrate
  The birth-day of the Church.

Although is seen no lambent flame,
  No rushing sounds are heard ;
Our strength is in Thy saving name,
  Our guidance in Thy word.

Weak and defenceless, lo ! we wait,
  The promise from on high ;
And with our tongues and hearts elate,
  Thy name to magnify.

Thy truth shall then the sinful turn,
    And set the captive free;
And like a guiding lamp, shall burn
    And shine from sea to sea.

WHITSUNDAY. No. 3.

"Nevertheless, I tell you the truth, it is expedient for you that I go away; for if I go not away, the *Comforter* will not come unto you; but if I depart, I will send him unto you." ST. JOHN, xvi. 7.

No longer mourn thy absent King;
    Again he comes to greet
His waiting saints; awake and sing,
    All hail the Paraclete!

He comes to teach the feeble mind,
    And guide the steps which stray;
To brace the lame, and on the blind
    To pour the light of day.

He comes to strengthen all who stand,
    To raise up those who fall;
In ev'ry Church, in ev'ry land,
    The Comforter of all.

Where'er the Church, in truth serene,
   Is built upon Thy Word,
The cloven tongues of fire are seen,
   The rushing wind is heard.

In ev'ry land Thy graces shine,
   Thou pure and heavenly Dove ;
From Zembla to the burning line,
   The Source of light and love.

O Holy Spirit, far and nigh,
   Thy heavn'ly grace distil,
And with the influence from on high
   Our hearts to fulness fill.

WHITSUNDAY. No. 4.

" And being assembled together with them, commanded them that they should not depart from Jerusalem, but wait for the promise of the Father, which, saith He, ye have heard of me." ACTS, i. 4.

ONCE more assembled in Thy name,
  Within Thy courts we stand ;
For Thou, O Christ, art still the same,
  To promise and command.

Once more in Pentecostal fire,
  Let Thy free Spirit strive ;
Once more our drooping hearts inspire,
  Our feeble hopes revive.

Give wisdom to Thy saints who teach,
  And make us meekly hear,
That the engrafted Word they preach
  May fill us with thy fear.

And let the Gospel's joyful sound
  Go forth from Zion's hill,
And to the earth's remotest bound,
  Thy glorious Kingdom fill.

9

To Thee our prayers and alms we bring,
  Thy praise shall be our theme ;
And soon the Morian's land shall sing,
  MESSIAH REIGNS SUPREME !

MONDAY IN WHITSUN WEEK.

"And they of the circumcision who believed were astonished, as many as came with Peter, because that on the Gentiles also was poured out the gift of the Holy Ghost." ACTS, x. 15.

No longer shall the tribes complain,
No longer mourn the hidden lore,
The mystic vail is rent in twain,
And Jew and Gentile are no more.

No longer shall the pilgrim stray,
Or seek in vain the Lord to know ;
For now to guide him on the way,
The Spirit shall before him go.

No longer shall the sinner shun
The throne of Grace in time of need ;
Our Great High Priest has access won,
And ever lives to intercede.

Beneath Thy wing, O Heav'nly Dove,
The law has lost its vengeful ire ;
And Jew and Gentile meet in love,
Amidst the Pentecostal fire.

Pour out, O Lord, the Holy Ghost,
And by the pow'r of second birth,
Add daily to thy savèd host,
Of all the suff'ring tribes of earth.

TUESDAY IN WHITSUN WEEK.

"When the Apostles who were at Jerusalem heard that Samaria had received the word of God, they sent unto them Peter and John ; who when they were come down, prayed for them, that they might receive the Holy Ghost." ACTS, viii. 14, 15.

COME, Holy Spirit, from above,
And by Thy pow'r divine,
Baptize us with the fire of love,*
And make us wholly Thine.

* Acts, i. 5.

O take us for Thy dwelling place ;
   The mind of Christ instil ;
And help us, by Thy saving grace,
   To know and do Thy will.

Thy Church replenish and restore,
   To yield her large increase,
And make the people more and more
   To grow in grace and peace.

So shall Thy Church with praise resound,
   In glory to Thy name ;
And we to all the world around,
   Thy mercy will proclaim.

TRINITY SUNDAY. No. 1.

"There are Three that bear record in heaven, the Father, the Word,
and the Holy Ghost : and these Three are One." 1 JOHN, v. 7.

FROM home to earth's remotest bound,
Let the Creator's praise resound ;
" Let the Redeemer's name be sung,
In ev'ry land, by ev'ry tongue."

Compose and swell your anthems high,
For Him who made the earth and sky,
Who gave the day its glorious light,
And gemm'd the forehead of the night.

Give glory to the Eternal Son,
Whose arm our great salvation won;
Who died that He might sins efface,
And lives to crown a ransom'd race.

O let your notes be soft and sweet,
To magnify the Paraclete,
By whom we breathe our vital breath,
Our guide in life, our peace in death.

All adoration be to Thee,
In Essence One, in Person Three;
Hidden and yet reveal'd to prove,
That " God is Light, " and " God is Love."

9*

TRINITY SUNDAY. No. 2.

THE secrets of Thy will, O Lord,
  Exceed our keenest search ;
Thy judgments in the world abroad,
  Thy counsels in the Church.

The ways and works of God excel
  The wisdom of the earth ;
No thought can reach, no tongue can tell,
  The myst'ry of their birth.

Like the inconstant winds conceal'd,
  We cannot find their source ;
Nor is the future track reveal'd,
  Of their predestined course.

And yet, mysterious Lord, Thy will
  With mercy is enlarg'd ;
And all designs of good and ill
  Are with salvation charg'd.

TRINITY SUNDAY. No. 3.

CREATION.

PRAISE to the Lord, our God and King,
In songs of gladness let us sing ;
Recount His love, record His name,
And spread abroad His matchless fame.

Praise to the Lord, whose word alone
Spread out and gemm'd the starry zone,
At whose command chaotic night
To order sprang, and it was light.

Praise to the Lord, who gave us breath,
And still preserves our souls from death ;
Who made the valleys bloom and bear,
And with his goodness crowns the year.

Praise to the Lord, the Lord alone,
Praise to the Lord, whose name is One ; *
Praise to the Righteous Branch and Rod,†
Praise to the Victor Son of God.

* Deut. vi. 4 ; Mark, xii. 29.   † Isaiah, xi. 1.

TRINITY SUNDAY. No. 4.
REDEMPTION.

PRAISE to the Lord, who by His Son,
Salvation for the world has won;
Who bore our sins, our sorrows brav'd,
That we might live redeem'd and sav'd.

Praise to the Lord, who reigns on high,
And in the mansions of the sky,
As promised, will the place prepare,
For his redeem'd to meet Him there.

Praise to the Lord, who when withdrawn
From earth, left not his Church forlorn;
And now to make his work complete,
Sends to our souls the *Paraclete*.

Praise to the Lord, the Lord alone,
Praise to the Lord, the only Son,
Praise to the Lord, the Spirit free,*
One Lord and God eternally.

* And stablish us with Thy free Spirit.   PSALM li. 12.

FIRST SUNDAY AFTER TRINITY. No. 1.

As passing days their sorrows bring,
　And turn the tide of peace,
Our souls to Thee, O Saviour, cling,
　And groan for their release.

As through the scenes of earth we roam,
　Our eyes are fix'd above,
On heav'n, our haven and our home,
　The realm of light and love —

Where Christ our Saviour reigns supreme,
　And sorrow finds no place,
And everlasting glories beam
　Upon a ransom'd race.

Forever guarded from offence,
　There all our strife shall cease ;
The Lord our Rock, our sure defence,
　And citadel of peace.

There, join'd to Christ their living head,
  The faithful dead are blest;
The sorrowful are comforted,
  The weary are at rest.

FIRST SUNDAY AFTER TRINITY.   No. 2.

"But Abraham said, Son, remember that thou in thy life-time receivedst thy good things, and likewise Lazarus evil things ; but now he is comforted, and thou art tormented."   ST. LUKE, xvi. 25.

REMEMBER ! O that word is fraught
  With sorrow and with fear ;
And bids us think, while we have thought,
  Upon our life-time here.

Remember ! O that word recalls
  A thousand scenes of pain,
And like a shroud of darkness falls
  On pleasure and on gain.

And can it be, that those who dwell
  In ease, with plenty bless'd,
Shall find their portion fix'd in hell,
  Tormented and distress'd ?

To cry with unavailing grief,
  And find no answering voice,
Save that denial of relief,
  Remember, 't was thy choice!

O may Thy terrors, gracious Lord,
  Persuade us now to give
A willing audience to Thy word,
  And serve Thee while we live.

SECOND SUNDAY AFTER TRINITY.

"Still there is room."   St. Luke, xiv. 16.

Room at the Feast! and Christ is there,
  To welcome all who come;
" *Still there is room*," and all may share
  Their Father's board and home.

Room at the Feast! though thousands press
  To meet the Saviour's call,
" *Still there is room*," and Christ shall bless
  His Marriage Festival.

Room at the Feast! and ev'ry race
  Acceptance there may find;
Fill up the room, there still is space
  For maim'd, and halt, and blind.

O Lord, the riches of Thy grace
  Are furnishèd in love;
O may we find a festal place
  Within Thy courts above;

There with Thy plenteous mercy blest,
  The Bridal song to sing,
And in the wedding garment dress'd,
  Hail our anointed King.

THIRD SUNDAY AFTER TRINITY.

"There is joy in the presence of the angels of God, over one sinner that repenteth." St. Luke, xv. 10.

As through this world of pains and fears,
  By devious steps we roam,
To heav'n we look, through blinding tears,
  Our Father's house and home.

There angels strong his face admire,*
  And keep their watch and ward;
And minister in flaming fire,
  Our steps to guide and guard.†

They soothe us in our hours of pain,‡
  Recall us when we stray;
And when on pleasure bent, or gain,
  They meet us in the way.§

O Lord of men and angels too,
  Combine us in thy love,
That we on earth Thy will may do,
  As done by them above.

O turn our thoughts to that bright throng,
  Our failing steps restore,
And make the angelic theme of song,
  " One savèd sinner more !"

* St. Matth. xviii. 10.   † Heb. i. 7, 14.   ‡ St. Luke, xxii. 43.
§ Numbers, xxii. 22.

10

FOURTH SUNDAY AFTER TRINITY.

O LORD, on our departed days,
   With shuddering hearts we look;
To know that all our works and ways,
   Are noted in Thy Book.

O, who can tell the vast amount
   Of sins inserted there;
Or who shall render the account,
   And yet escape despair!

The sins of youth and riper years
   Our stooping souls oppress;
In vain our pray'rs, in vain our tears,
   To save us from distress.

O Saviour Christ, Thy pard'ning love
   The heaving breast shall calm;
Thy precious blood our guilt remove
   And keep us from alarm.

O Lamb of God, beneath Thy Cross
  Our sins and sorrows cease ;
And all the world we count but loss,
  Comparèd with Thy peace.

FIFTH SUNDAY AFTER TRINITY.

WHEN toss'd upon a troubled sea,
And the wild storm in anger blows,
Thou art the *Rock*, beneath Thy lee
The shatter'd bark may find repose.

With fierce temptation sorely press'd,
And passion raging in the breast,
Thou art the *Tower*, and within
We find the safe escape from sin.

Whene'er in devious paths we stray,
When clouds and darkness cast their gloom,
Thou art the *Light* upon the way,
That leads us to our peaceful home.

The clouds disperse, the whirlwinds cease,
Before Thy potent words of peace :
" *Fear not ;* " we feel no more alarm :
" *Be still ;* " and all around is calm.

When thoughts of sin and burning tears,
Pour on our souls a 'whelming flood ;
Beneath the Cross we cast our fears,
And find our peace in Jesus' blood.

When the last fiery storm shall blow,
When the last waves of wrath shall flow,
Then let us find a safe retreat,
Before a Saviour's mercy-seat.

SIXTH SUNDAY AFTER TRINITY.

CITIES OF REFUGE.

"And of these cities which ye shall give, six cities shall ye have for refuge." NUMBERS, xxxv. 13.

WHERE'ER I turn mine eyes,
Where'er my footsteps tread,
I hear the victim's cries.
On every wind, in baleful notes,
The voice of accusation floats,
And fills my soul with dread.

How shall I hide the stain,
What path for safety take,
What place of refuge gain —
To make a sure and peaceful home,
Where the Avenger cannot come,
His burning wrath to slake?

"Refuge"! at ev'ry turn
The weary soul elates,
Its letters breathe and burn;

10*

The path is plain, the city free,
Gird up thy loins, my soul, and flee,
   And live within its gates.

   From ev'ry danger free,
   And safe from ev'ry harm,
   I yield myself to Thee,
My God, to serve Thee night and day,
And work in faith, and watch and pray,
   Until the last alarm.

   In vain shall foes assail,
   In vain th' Avenger search,
   No weapon shall prevail;
With bread bestow'd and water sure,
Refresh'd, and strengthen'd, and secure,
   Within Thy holy Church.

   In peace and love I rest,
   'Till Christ shall come again,
   And with Him all the blest,
To sing within Thy courts above,
The anthem of eternal love,
   " The enmity is slain."

SEVENTH SUNDAY AFTER TRINITY.

"For the wages of sin is death; but the gift of God is eternal life, through Jesus Christ our Lord." ROM. vi. 23.

AND shall we to our Lord and King
A life of less devotion bring,
Than that which in our former days
We gave to sin and sinful ways?

Unswerving then the course we ran,
Careless alike of God and man;
By Satan bound, through paths of ill
He led us captive at his will.

As, free from all restraint, we went
From wrong to wrong, on evil bent;
So make us now, with purpose true,
The ways of holiness pursue.

No longer from Thy paths we stray,
The former things are pass'd away;
Enjoy'd, they taint our vital breath,
The fruit is shame, the end is death.

Avert, O Lord, this dreadful doom ;
Though earn'd, let not the wages come ;
But spread abroad the Living Word,
Thine own great gift through Christ our Lord.

EIGHTH SUNDAY AFTER TRINITY.

WHILE struggling in a world of sin,
  To Thee, O Lord, we fly ;
With wars without and fears within,
  On Thee our souls rely.

When wrestling with the foe in vain,
  By passion overthrown,
Let Thy Free Spirit break the chain,
  And seal us for Thine own.

O " Abba Father ! " that sweet word
  Shall calm each boding fear ;
And witness silently though heard,
  Thy saving help is near.

O God, by whom all creatures live,
From bondage set us free ;
Keep back all hurtful things, and give
The grace to trust in Thee.

And like the trees that bloom and bear,
When water'd from above,
Our lives from henceforth shall declare
The influence of Thy love.

NINTH SUNDAY AFTER TRINITY. No. 1.

"Lord of all pow'r and might,"
On Thee for aid we call,
To guide our feeble steps aright,
And save us when we fall.

Unless Thy grace prevail,
No good thing we fulfil ;
Without Thy saving grace, we fail
To do Thy sacred will.

In vain we pass the sea,
If still in sin we rove ;
In vain refreshing streams from Thee,
If unrefreshed with love.

In vain the baptist's tide
Shall open all its springs, ·
If from the Rock we turn aside,
And lust for evil things.

When tempted to betray
The sacred name we bear,
Or when our careless footsteps stray,
O God, awake our fear ;

And shield us with Thy hand ;
On Thee our hopes rely ;
With Thee the tempter we withstand,
Without Thee we must die.

NINTH SUNDAY AFTER TRINITY. No. 2.

" And after the fire, a still small voice." 1 KINGS, xix. 12.

'T is not the thunder's crash,
And lightning's livid glare,
That mark the presence of the Lord,
And make us feel Him near.

'T is not the rending earth,
And storms that sweep amain,
That stay the sinner on his path,
And turn him back again.

But still small notes of love,
Which o'er the heart-strings sweep,
Which turn the thoughts to things above,
And soothe us while we weep.

They cheer us while we stand ;
They warn us when we stray ;
They wake the heart to God's command,
And force us to obey.*

* *" The love Christ of constraineth us."* 2 COR. v. 14.

With Thy sure counsel blest,
Our fears and sorrows cease ;
In Thee, the weary soul finds rest,
The pardon'd sinner peace.

TENTH SUNDAY AFTER TRINITY.

This life is but a fleeting shade,
A flow'r that only blooms to fade,
With all the joy it brings.
For all the pageant of a day,
O let not our affections stray,
From heav'n and heav'nly things.

With house to house and field to field,
Abundance can no safety yield,
Nor all we have or crave ;
All earthly things contract their span,
And only leave the dying man
Possession of a grave.

On things above our hearts shall stay,
The things which never pass away,
  Which never wane or die;
Where saints inherit ev'rything,
And Jesus sits th' Eternal King,
  At God's right hand on high.

ELEVENTH SUNDAY AFTER TRINITY.

"And the Publican standing afar off would not lift up so much as his eyes unto heaven, but smote his breast, saying, God be merciful to me a sinner." St. Luke, xviii. 13.

A THOUSAND sins our hearts defile,
  And fill them with distrust:
Lord, we abhor ourselves as vile,
  Repentant in the dust.*

Beneath the glance of Thy pure eye,
  Our sins are brought to light;
Though hidden from ourselves, they lie
  Reveal'd to Thy sight.

                    * Job, xlii. 6.

For righteous works we urge no plea,
  We ask for no reward;
As sinners we appeal to Thee;
  Be merciful, O Lord!

Be merciful, our hearts revive,
  To yield Thee service meet;
And make us humbly, while we live,
  To worship at Thy feet.

TWELFTH SUNDAY AFTER TRINITY.

ALTHOUGH our hearts with guilt are stung,
Although we plead with stamm'ring tongue,
Still let our feeble pray'rs prevail,
And let not Thy compassion fail.

Before we ask, an answer Thou
Hast sent to soothe our fev'rish brow;
Before we can for mercy crave,
Thy hand is stretchèd out to save.

Pour down upon us, loving Lord,
The blessings of Thy works and Word ;
Give to us all we need to live,
And our alarming sins forgive.*

" *Ephphatha* " *!* speak the potent word,
Our ears shall hear ; our tongues be heard ;
And evermore Thy praise shall tell,
" *All things,* " O Lord, " *Thou hast done well.* "†

THIRTEENTH SUNDAY AFTER TRINITY.

" Then said Jesus unto him, Go and do thou likewise." St. Luke, x. 37.

" HEREIN *is love* " *!* O matchless love,
Which gave the Son from heav'n above,
   To dwell on earth with man ;
With man to live in suff'ring state,
And then his sins to expiate,
   To die beneath a bann.‡

* Collect for the day.   † St. Mark, vii. 34 — 87.
‡ 1 John, iv. 10.   Gal. iii. 13.

He found us by the way-side, maim'd,
By sin disrob'd, by Satan claim'd,
  Left friendless and distress'd ;
He heal'd our wounds with oil and wine,
And took us with His care divine,
  Within His Church to rest.

To emulate Thy loving life,
O Lord subdue our sinful strife,
  Our souls with love inflame ;
And let Thy great example move,
Our hearts their gratitude to prove,
  To go and do the same.

FOURTEENTH SUNDAY AFTER TRINITY. No. 1.

"And they lifted up their voices and said, Jesus, Master, have mercy on us." St. Luke, xvii. 13.

OPPRESS'D with grief, by sin defil'd,
By Satan tempted and beguil'd,
To Thee, O Saviour, we repair,
That in Thy mercy we may share;
 Jesus, Master, hear our cry,
 Hear and save us, or we die!

When darkness overhangs our path,
When threaten'd with impending wrath,
When overpress'd with toil we droop,
When sorrow makes the heart to stoop;
 Jesus, hear our plaintive voice,
 Hear and make our hearts rejoice!

When by Thy vengeful arrow torn,
With shame and anguish overborne;
When sins, which have in darkness lain,
Rise up reproachfully again;
 Jesus, hear our contrite prayer,
 Hear and save us from despair!

11*

When friends, in fear and silence, tread
Around a sinner's dying bed;
When, trembling on the fleeting breath,
For mercy is the cry of death;
   As we sink into the grave,
    Jesus, Master, hear and save!

Redeem'd and cleans'd, our souls will burn,
To give Thee thanks at Thy return;
When myriads shall Thy mercies own,
And cast their crowns before Thy throne;
   Hear, O King, the thankful song
    Sung by all Thy ransom'd throng.

FOURTEENTH SUNDAY AFTER TRINITY. No. 2.

AFTER A BOUNTIFUL HARVEST.

"He reserveth unto us the appointed weeks of the harvest." JERE-
MIAH, v. 24.*

O LORD, Thy promises prevail,
  Seed-time and harvest never fail,
    Our labors to repay;

* Lesson for the day.

The ripen'd fruits our fields adorn,
And valleys standing thick with corn,
  Thy bounteous love display.

The clouds drop fatness on the fields ;
Enrich'd, the soil abundance yields,
  The earth is stor'd with food ;
At Thy command the teeming ground
Its plenty pours on all around,
  And all is fill'd with good.

To Thee, O Lord, our God and King,
The tribute of our love we bring,
  Our grateful notes we raise ;
And while the valleys laugh and sing,
Our tongues shall make Thy temple ring
  With th' anthem of our praise.

FIFTEENTH SUNDAY AFTER TRINITY. No. 1.

" Take no thought for the morrow." MATTH. vi. 34.

ALL that we have, O Lord, is Thine,
    And ev'ry passing hour,
Crown'd with Thy goodness, is the sign
    Of Thy protecting pow'r.

The flowers that in the valley spring,
    Our faithless hearts reprove ;
The birds that in the woodland sing,
    Remind us of Thy love.

Daily on us Thy mercies fall,
    And we will ask no more ;
To-morrow, if it come at all,
    Will bring its needful store.

O Lord, we seek for other dress,
    For other food we crave —
Thy Kingdom and Thy righteousness,
    Thy pow'r and will to save.

Thy promises our thoughts shall guide,
    And keep us from alarm ;
To-morrow shall itself provide
    A sure escape from harm.

FIFTEENTH SUNDAY AFTER TRINITY. No. 2.
AFTER AN UNPRODUCTIVE HARVEST.

"Your iniquities have turned away these things, and your sins have withholden good things from you." JEREMIAH, v. 25.

Thy will be done, O King,
    Whate'er that will ordain,
    Whatever ills it bring ;
Although the " *barren land and dearth* "
With famine overspread the earth,
    Our tongues shall not complain.

Thy will be done, O God ;
    Though stern Thy judgments be,
    Our lips shall kiss the rod ;
Although the fruits should fail, and all
The cattle perish in the stall,
    Our hearts shall trust in Thee.

Thy will be done, Most High ;
That will is good and just ;
On Thee our hopes rely :
All we desire and all we want,
We know 't is in Thy pow'r to grant,
And in that pow'r we trust.

Thy will be done ; once more,
Beneath the genial sun,
The earth shall yield its store ;
And we will lift our grateful voice,
In Thy salvation to rejoice.
Amen ! Thy will be done.*

FIFTEENTH SUNDAY AFTER TRINITY.   No. 3.

"But God forbid that I should glory, save in the Cross of our Lord Jesus
Christ, by whom the world is crucified unto me and I unto the world."
GAL. vi. 14.

SAV'D by the Cross, I feel its pow'r
To banish all my fears ;
It shines in ev'ry sadden'd hour,
The Iris in my tears.

* Habak. iii. 17, 18.

When borne upon the preacher's voice
  I hear its praises ring,
In Thy salvation I rejoice,
  My martyr'd Lord and King.

O God, forbid that I should boast,
  Save in this seal of heav'n ;
The sign of safety to the lost,
  The pledge of sins forgiv'n.

'T is in my heart, 't is in mine eye,
  It brings my tongue employ ;
It gives to pray'r its language high,
  It gives to praise its joy.

I see it on the sunny lawn,
  It is my song at night ;
It meets me at the op'ning dawn,
  And makes my darkness light.

No matter what the pain or loss ;
  While I have life and breath,
I 'll glory in th' uplifted Cross,
  And cling to it in death.

SIXTEENTH SUNDAY AFTER TRINITY.

" And when the Lord saw her, he had compassion on her, and said unto her, Weep not." St. Luke, vii. 13.*

It is a vale of tears,
In which we make our stay ;
A desert land of foes and fears,
Through which we force a way.

But in our hours of grief,
And on our dang'rous road ;
" *Weep not*," that word affords relief,
We know Thy voice, O Lord.

When friendless and distress'd,
In sickness and in pain ;
Or when by sorrows overpress'd,
We call for help in vain ;

When bending o'er the bier,
On which our lov'd ones lie ;
" *Weep not*," the blessed word we hear,
And ev'ry tear is dry.

* Gospel for the day.

And when convinc'd of sin,
The very heart is riven,
The same consoling word within,
Shall whisper " *all forgiv'n.*"

All, all will pass away,
Our sorrows and our fears ;
" *Weep not* " ! once more the Lord shall say,
And wipe away all tears.*

SEVENTEENTH SUNDAY AFTER TRINITY.

"There is one body and one spirit, even as ye are called in one hope of
your calling : one Lord, one faith, one baptism, one God and Father of
all, who is above all, and through all, and in you all." EPHESIANS, iv. 4,
5, 6.

MYRIADS within Thy Church agree,
Are one in heart and soul ;
Join'd in one body, Lord, to Thee,
One Spirit guides the whole.

* Rev. vii. 17.

12

" *One Lord*," in whose benignant smile
  We share the joys of earth ;
" *One Lord*," by whose prolific Word,
  We have our second birth.

" *One Faith*," by which alone we claim
  Companionship in heav'n ;
" *One Faith*," through which in Jesus' name,
  Our sins are all forgiv'n.

" *One Font*," which holds the sacred flood,
  In which we all may lave ;
" *One Font*," enrich'd with Jesus' blood,
  With pow'r to cleanse and save.

" *One Lord and Father* " of us all,
  In whom we live and move ;
O give us grace to dwell as one,
  In lowliness and love —

And make us in Thy love abide,
  And all contention cease ;
And let Thy gentle Spirit guide
  Our feet in paths of peace.

EIGHTEENTH SUNDAY AFTER TRINITY.

"To them who believe, He is precious."   1 Peter, ii. 7.

On Thee, O Christ, we build our faith,
  On Thee our hopes erect ;
Thou art the Stone in Zion laid,
  The Precious, the Elect.

More precious than the costly balm,
  The balsam tree distils,
Or golden treasures that enrich
  The everlasting hills.*

More precious than the priceless pearls,
  Which merchant-princes own ;
Or rubies dug from earth, to gem
  The kingly crown and throne.

The precious things of heav'n and earth,
  And in th' unfathom'd sea ;
The jewels and the precious fruit,†
  All yield in worth to Thee.

* Deut. xxxii. 13, 14, 15.   † James, v. 7.

Precious to God the Lord's Elect,
  The Righteous Branch and Rod,*
And precious to believing souls
  Thy blood, O Lamb of God.†

NINETEENTH SUNDAY AFTER TRINITY.

" And Jesus seeing their faith, saith unto the sick of the palsy, Son, be
of good cheer, thy sins be forgiven thee." St. Matth. ix. 2.‡

CORRUPT, and weak, and self-condemn'd,
Before Thy mercy-seat we lie ;
With shame and sorrow overwhelm'd,
To Thee for mercy, Lord, we cry.

We will not cease to pray, unheal'd,
We cannot rest, while unforgiv'n ;
We dare not go, while unrepeal'd
Thy sentence bars the way to heav'n.

* Isaiah, xi. 1.   † 1 Peter, i. 19.
                ‡ Gospel for the day.

O may Thy Spirit rule our hearts,
Our sins remove, our lusts subdue ;
And let it cleanse our inward parts,
Our palsied frames and minds renew.

Thou hast forgiv'n ! absolv'd and heal'd,
Thy word we hear, Thy peace receive ;
Our souls renew'd, restor'd and seal'd,
No more the Holy Ghost shall grieve.*

No longer by our sins enthrall'd,
In quiet confidence we stay ;
No more with threaten'd woes appall'd,
We calmly wait the Judgment Day.

* Ephesians, iv. 80.

12*

TWENTIETH SUNDAY AFTER TRINITY.

"Wherewith shall I come before the Lord, and bow myself before the
High God?" MICAH, vi. 6.*

OH! how shall we appear,
What off'ring shall we bring,
Or how with confidence draw near
To our offended King?

What can his wrath endure?
What can for sins atone?
Or what to sinful man ensure
Acceptance at His throne?

In vain shall beasts be slain,
The chief of all our store;
Rivers of oil we shall in vain
Upon His altars pour.

Our first-born though we gave
To die in flood or flame,
Not e'en this sacrifice could save
Our guilty souls from blame.

* Lesson for the day.

O, Saviour, Thou alone,
Canst draw us to Thy seat;
None else can for our sins atone,
And make our off'ring meet.

O clothe us with Thy Grace,
That in the realms above,
We may with joy behold Thy face
And share Thy boundless love.

TWENTY-FIRST SUNDAY AFTER TRINITY.

"My brethren, be strong in the Lord, and in the power of His might. Put on the whole armor of God, that ye may be able to stand against the wiles of the Devil." EPHESIANS, vi. 10, 11.*

WEAK and unarm'd, to Thee we fly,
"Lord of all pow'r and might";
Send us assistance from on high,
And teach our hands to fight.

* Epistle for the day.

Our strength in ev'ry dang'rous hour,
  Our shield from ev'ry foe;
And in Thy armor clad, no pow'r
  Our souls shall overthrow.

Th' imperious strife which flesh may wage,
  Thy wisdom shall control,
And all the sinful lusts which rage
  And war against the soul.

Thy Word the tempter's pow'r shall scathe,
  The tempter's wiles repel;
And blunted on the shield of faith,
  Shall fall the darts of hell.

Unwearied, we will watch and pray,
  Until the strife is past,
That, through Thy saving strength, we may
  Be conquerors at last.

141

TWENTY-SECOND SUNDAY AFTER TRINITY.

" Forgive, and ye shall be forgiven." St. Luke, vi. 37.

O holy Saviour of mankind,
The graces of Thy word impart ;
Inspire me with Thy patient mind,
And write Thy precepts on my heart.

Teach me the ills of life to share ;
Teach me in peace with all to live ;
As Thou forbearest, to forbear ;
As Thou forgivest, to forgive.

Let me no angry passion bear,
No vengeful thoughts my heart possess ;
That they who hate, my love may share,
And them who curse me, I may bless.

O, by Thy tears in sorrow shed
O'er guilty Judah's threaten'd woes,
And by the prayer in anguish said
For man who mock'd Thy dying throes—

Fill up my heart with love divine,
The love that came to earth from heav'n;
And make Thy great example mine,
That I forgive and be forgiven.

TWENTY-THIRD SUNDAY AFTER TRINITY.

"For our conversation is in heaven : from whence also we look for the
Saviour, the Lord Jesus Christ ; who shall change our vile body, that it
may be fashioned like unto His glorious body."   PHIL. iii. 20, 21.*

JESUS, withdrawn from mortal sight,
    To mortals still 't is given
To speak to Thee, enthron'd in light,
    To look for Thee from heav'n.

Although the scenes of earth from hence
    Present a glorious show,
They shall not bend our hearts to sense,
    Or chain our thoughts below.

* Epistle for the day.

Awhile bedoom'd amidst the foes
 Of Thy dear Cross to move,
Still heav'n its reflex glory throws
 On those who share his love.

Though cloth'd awhile in mortal guise,
 By mortal sin derang'd,
The day will come when we shall rise,
 With this " *vile body* " chang'd.

Chang'd, and made like the Son of God,
 Beatified and crown'd ;
While all His foes beneath His rod,
 Are in perdition drown'd.

TWENTY-FOURTH SUNDAY AFTER TRINITY.

"Giving thanks unto the Father who hath made us meet to be parta
kers of the inheritance of the saints in light." COL. i. 12.*

LESS than the least of saints,
 Before Thy throne we kneel ;
O Jesus, hear our sad complaints,
 And saving grace reveal.

* Epistle for the day.

Though tied and bound with sin,
Our hopes are fix'd on Thee;
O Saviour, break the galling chains,
Absolve and set us free.

Give wisdom from above,
And strengthen us with might,
To know Thy pure and perfect will,
And do that will aright.

Thy truth shall make us free,
Thy grace our hearts console;
Thy garment's hem is fraught with health,
Thy Word shall make us whole.*

By Thee our stainèd robes
Are cleansèd and made white,
With all our pristine pow'rs restor'd,
To dwell with saints in light.

* See Gospel for the day.   Matth. ix.

SUNDAY NEXT BEFORE ADVENT.

"Stir up, we beseech Thee, the wills of Thy faithful people."
COLLECT FOR THE DAY.

STIR up our wills with grace divine,
And make them to resemble Thine;
That we may work Thy works, O Lord,
And reap at last Thy great reward,
When Thou shalt sit upon Thy throne,
And make Thy Righteousness our own.

Stir up our thoughts, so apt to sleep,
While we our solemn vigil keep;
And from the past our minds recall
The mem'ry of each guilty fall,
And stretch beyond the present hour,
When Thou shalt come again in pow'r.

Stir up Thy strength, and come again
To earth with all Thy countless train;

13

From pole to pole Thy glory spread,
Reclothe the quick, revive the dead;
And all our new-born pow'rs shall bless
The Lord, our Strength and Righteousness.*

ST. ANDREW'S DAY.

" Wherefore, seeing that we also are compassed about with so great a
cloud of witnesses, let us lay aside every weight and the sin which doth
so easily beset us, and let us run with patience the race that is set before
us." HEB. xii. 1.

WE cherish in our hearts, O Lord,
    The mem'ry of the just;
In silence they proclaim Thy Word,
    Though mingl'd with the dust.

They bid us ev'ry weight displace,
    Besetting sins to shun,
And run with patience in the race
    Which They on earth have run.

* Jeremiah, xxiii. 6.

They hover round us like a cloud,
　The witnesses of grace ;
And call us from their blest abode,
　To share their dwelling place.

They teach us with unfailing heart,
　On Jesus to rely —
In life like them to do our part,
　Like them in faith to die.

O Jesus, Lord, we count but loss,
　All things for Thee alone,
That we may glory in Thy Cross,
　And sit upon Thy Throne.

ST. THOMAS THE APOSTLE.

"Jesus saith unto him, Thomas, because thou hast seen me thou hast believed ; blessed are they that have not seen and yet believed." St. John, xx. 29.

Assail'd by doubts, to Thee, O Lord,
　We fly for sure relief ;
And while the Gospel we believe,
　Still help our unbelief.*

* Mark, ix. 24.

Our ears are deaf, our eyes are dim,
   Our hearts are hard and cold;
Then let the promis'd Paraclete,
   Thy mysteries unfold.

We crave no surer Word to teach,
   No surer sign to prove —
Thy truth divine, Thy saving grace,
   And everlasting love.

" *We walk by faith,*" and Thy sure Word
   From age to age endures;
And to th' *unseeing* who believe,
   Thy blessedness secures.

CONVERSION OF ST. PAUL. No. 1.

"And as he journeyed he came near Damascus: and suddenly there shined round about him a light from heaven: And he fell to the earth, and heard a voice saying unto him, Saul, Saul, why persecutest thou me?"

ACTS, ix. 4.

THE awful voice and radiant fire
    Fall on the oppressor's path,
With words of love and signs of ire
    To intercept his wrath.

Praise to the Lord, who keeps the feet
    Of the oppress'd from harm;
Provides us with a safe retreat,
    And saves us from alarm.

When tempted from Thy truth we stray,
    Or wander into ill,
O meet and warn us on the way,
    And change our froward will.

Our souls to Thee convert and call,
    Direct and guide our choice,
And make us, like Thy servant *Paul*,
    Obedient to Thy voice.

13*

CONVERSION OF ST. PAUL. No. 2.

" Who was before a blasphemer, and a persecutor, and injurious : but I obtained mercy, because I did it ignorantly in unbelief." 1 Tim. i. 13.

AND is this he, whose baleful breath
Was fraught with threat'ning and with death ;
Whose furious zeal and iron rod
Made havoc of the Church of God ?

'T is he, who erst with scornful eye
Look'd on the Christians doom'd to die ;
Who ruthless 'midst the carnage stood,
The shedder of a martyr's blood.

'T is he, who *once* on mischief bent,
From Judah to Damascus sent ;
Now chosen to convey the Word
And knowledge of th' Incarnate Lord —

Through Gentile tribes His name to spread,
Once slain, now risen from the dead,
And to remotest ages prove
The pattern of forbearing love.*

* 1 Tim i. 16.

O Source of good, O Pow'r supreme,
Light from the Light pour out astream,
Arrest our steps where'er we stray,
And teach and aid us to obey.

Our stubborn hearts with grace instil,
And bend us to Thy blessed will ;
Remove the film from off our eyes,
And make us to salvation wise.

PRESENTATION OF CHRIST IN THE TEMPLE.

"They brought Him to Jerusalem to present him to the Lord." Acts,
i. 26.

Who to the temple comes forlorn,
    Lowly and yet ador'd ?
It is the pure and virgin born,
    Presented to the Lord.

He comes, the helpless child of earth,
    In human nature dress'd ;
Hail, favor'd one who gave Him birth,
    Among all women blest !

To Thee, O Saviour Christ, alone,
  Adoring hearts we raise;
With Thee no mortal shares the throne,
  No angel shares the praise.

O Child of man, in glory seen,
  God with our manhood blent,*
Our hearts, by Thee made pure and clean,
  To Thee we now present.

ST. MATTHIAS'S DAY.

"And the lot fell upon Matthias, and he was numbered with the eleven Apostles." ACTS, i. 26.

LORD, for the glory of thy name,
The promise of Thy pow'r we claim,
For those whom now Thy Church empow'rs
To guard her gates and watch her tow'rs.

As with the Pentecostal fire,
Their hearts with grace divine inspire,
With knowledge clear their minds endue,
And to their mission make them true.

* St. John, i. 14.

Instruct them, Lord, Thy Word to teach,
And give them boldness when they preach;
And make our hearts within us burn
With hope and joy for Thy return.

O Christ, before Thy throne above,
Their work and *our* esteem approve,
And in Thy presence let us share
The full salvation promis'd there.

THE ANNUNCIATION OF THE BLESSED VIRGIN MARY.

"And behold thou shalt conceive in thy womb, and bring forth a son, and shalt call his name Jesus."   St. Luke, i. 31.

THE mystic roll is seal'd,
Unstrung the prophets' lyres,
When, lo! the time of times reveal'd,
To fulness fill'd, expires.

A thousand saints believe
The message sent from heav'n;
A virgin shall a son conceive,
Born, but divinely giv'n.

Hush! 't is a voice so sweet,
It cannot be of earth;
It comes the lowly maid to greet,
And tell Messiah's birth.

Cloth'd with the light, he stands
The herald of the skies;
And charg'd by God's supreme commands,
Hail! favor'd one, he cries.

Thee shall the nations bless,
And fame to Thee accord,
And to the latest age confess
The mother of the Lord.

Mary, we call the blest,
But CHRIST alone we love;
She with the righteous dead shall rest,
He reigns in bliss above.

Though born of mortal race,
Unknown to mortal shame,
No stains of mortal sin deface
The pure *Immanuel's* name.

O may His grace adorn,
And raise our souls to heav'n ;
To us the Child of man is born,
To us the Son is giv'n.

ST. MARK'S DAY.

"And he gave some, apostles ; and some, prophets ; and some, evange-
lists ; and some, pastors and teachers ; for the perfecting of the saints, for
the work of the ministry, for the edifying of the body of Christ." EPH.
iv. 11, 12.

THY Holy Church, O gracious Lord,
From age to age we trace ;
The keeper of Thy precious Word,
And treasure-house of grace.

From earth withdrawn, Thou still art near,
Thy saints to bless and teach,
And still Thy gentle voice we hear
Whene'er Thy servants preach.

On these look down, O Prince of Peace,
  In mercy from Thy throne,
And make their ministry of grace
  Effective as Thy own.

Once more upon this chosen band,
  O breathe Thy grace divine,
That by Thy inspiration fann'd,
  Their light may burn and shine.

O send them forth to ev'ry place,
  With messages of love,
And give them souls redeem'd by grace,
  To fill Thy Church above.

ST. PHILIP AND ST. JAMES'S DAY.

"Jesus saith unto him, I am the way, the truth and the life." ST. JOHN, xiv. 6.

WHERE, in this world of sin and woe,
  Shall we escape the strife ?
To whom, O gracious Saviour, go ?
  Thou hast eternal life !

In Thee both grace and mercy shine,
   Reflected from above;
We see Thy Father's face in Thine,
   We know Him in Thy love.

A thousand foes our steps betray,
   In devious paths to roam;
But Thou, O Saviour, art the way,
   To reach our Father's home.

And when misled by lures of sense,
   Where'er we turn our eyes,
Thou art the Truth to sweep away
   " The refuges of lies."*

Thou art the Way, the Truth, the Life;
   On Thee our hopes rely,
To find, prepar'd with blessings rife,
   Our Father's house on high.

* Isaiah, xxviii. 15.

14

ST. BARNABAS THE APOSTLE.

"The son of consolation." Acts, iv. 36.

We bless Thy holy name, O Lord,
For all the comforts shed abroad
  By ministers of grace;
For all Thy servants sent to preach,
To strengthen, warn, console, and teach,
  In ev'ry time and place.

Continue, Lord, Thy Church to fill
With Pastors, moulded to Thy will,
  And to Thy service sworn;
That with the comforts they possess,
They may the broken-hearted bless,
  And comfort all who mourn.

Surround them with Thy promis'd pow'r,
That on the contrite they may show'r
  A stream of gladness down;
Endue them all with sacred fire,
And give them precious souls for hire,
  To be their joy and crown.

ST. JOHN BAPTIST'S DAY. No. 1.

" At that time Herod the tetrach heard of the fame of Jesus, and said unto his servants, This is John the Baptist : he is risen from the dead, and therefore mighty works do show forth themselves in him." St. Matth xiv. 1, 2.

A THOUSAND lights their radiance throw
On plumèd helm and jewell'd brow,
   In Judah's regal hall ;
And dance and song with joy invest
Each " high estate " that night a guest
   At Herod's festival.

With lightsome step and graceful mien,
The daughter of the lawless queen
   Has charm'd the monarch's eyes ;
" *Ask what thou wilt* " — my kingdom share !
" *Give me the Baptist's head* " ; — the prayer
   Is heard ; the Baptist dies !

And all is still ! the guests are gone,
Herod the King is left alone,
   O'erwhelm'd with boding fears :
He sees a ghost in passing things ;
And in each sound that terror brings,
   The cry of murder hears.

And when the fame of Jesus flies,
" *'Tis John*"! the startled monarch cries,
  " *He is risen from the dead;* "
I smote him when in love he spake,
And now he comes with pow'r, to slake
  His vengeance on my head.

When Priests and Prophets speak the word,
Or when Thy " *still small voice* " is heard,
  Lord, make our hearts attent;
Subdue us with its accents bland,
And with Thy pow'r restrain the hand
  That is on mischief bent.

ST. JOHN BAPTIST'S DAY. No. 2.

"He was a burning and a shining light; and ye were willing for a sea
son to rejoice in his light." ST. JOHN, v. 35.

FREE from alarm, the martyrs sleep,
  No more they feel the oppressors' rod,
  No more in dungeons left to weep,
  The doom'd confessors of their God.

No longer made the scorner's jest,
No more unpitied left to die,
Among the dead in Christ they rest,
Safe in Thy care, O God, Most High!

Of prophets born, the greatest seal'd,
We hail the herald of the Son,
Who first the Lamb of God reveal'd,
Who first announc'd th' *Anointed One!*

Though doom'd the wrath of man to feel,
Though in a dungeon left to moan,
Though bow'd beneath the headsman's steel,
His warnings shook the Tetrarch's throne.

" A burning and a shining light,"
We still rejoice beneath its rays ;
His voice still guides our feet aright,
His dirge is still our thankful praise.

But greater is Thy witness, Lord,
And wider is Thy matchless fame ;
While grace and mercy in Thy Word,
Shed light and glory on Thy name.

14*

O, be to us a sun and shield,
To guide our feet and guard our path ;
And let Thy Spirit comfort yield,
If call'd to bear th' oppressor's wrath.

ST. PETER'S DAY.

"And Simon Peter answered and said, Thou art the Christ, the Son of
the living God."   ST. MATTH. xvi. 16.

" THOU *art the Christ*," the Holy One,
In whom the rays of Godhead beam,
The long-expected, only Son,
" Before all worlds " the Lord supreme.

Though cloth'd in flesh the child of man,
Of Jesse's house the Branch and Rod,*
None can Thy lofty lineage scan,
From everlasting Thou art God.

* Isaiah xi. 1.

" *Thou art the Christ* " : on this sure word
Thy Church is built, no more to fail ;
Redeem'd and purchas'd by Thy blood,
No weapon harms, no pow'rs prevail.

Thy precepts guide, Thy blood atones,
Daily be this confession made ;
Build up, build up, with living stones,
The strong foundation Thou hast laid.

" *Thou art the Christ* " : let grace descend
On all who watch and guard His tow'rs ;
And Thy supernal blessing send
To vindicate their sacred pow'rs.

ST. JAMES THE APOSTLE.

" Obey them that have the rule over you, and submit yourselves, for
they watch for your souls." HEBREWS, xiii. 17.

O LORD, Thy Spirit full and free,
Pour out on all who act for Thee ;
And make them watchful, wise, and bold,
To guide Thy flock and guard Thy fold.

Ambassadors from heav'n above,
They come with messages of love,
And to rebellious man proclaim
Peace and forgiveness in Thy name.

The watchmen of the Lord, they wait
To meet the foemen at the gate,
And at the first approach of harm,
To sound the trumpet and alarm.

Thousands, who in the forefront stood,
Have seal'd their witness with their blood ;*
But speak again, and countless hosts
Shall rise prepar'd to fill their posts.

To Thee, O thronèd Priest, we pray,
What they command may we obey ;
And to what they ordain as fit,
O give us meekness to submit.

* Per ignes ad cœlum.
BISHOP HOOKER's MOTTO.

ST. BARTHOLOMEW THE APOSTLE.

" Ye are they which have continued with me in my temptations ; and I
appoint unto you a kingdom, as my Father hath appointed unto me."
ST. LUKE, xxii. 28, 29.

O LORD, Thy saints in rapture deep,
Releas'd from toil, in Jesus sleep ;
And rest in hope that yet awhile,
And they shall wake beneath Thy smile.

Awhile they struggled in the cause
Of Jesus and His righteous laws ;
And sin resisting unto blood,
They sank beneath the whelming flood.

Though dead, we hear their welcome voice ;
It bids us in our woes rejoice,
And wait in patience for the hour
When Thou shalt come again in pow'r.

O come again, and with Thee bring
All saints Thy new-made song to sing,
Worthy the Lamb for sinners slain,
Welcome the King to earth again.

O may we learn to love Thy Word,
Which they have preach'd and we have heard;
That with them in the radiant skies,
We to appointed thrones may rise.

ST. MATTHEW THE APOSTLE.

"And as Jesus passed forth from thence, he saw a man, named Matthew, sitting at the receipt of custom; and he said unto him, Follow me. And he arose and followed him." ST. MATTH. ix. 9.

IN all the busy scenes of life,
    We turn, O Lord, to Thee,
And hear Thy word with promise rife,
    Arise and " follow me."

Not at the tribute seat alone,
    Not by a chosen band;
By ev'ry tribe Thy voice is known,
    'T is heard in ev'ry land.

'T is heard within the low retreat,
    Deep in the silent wood,
On tented fields where cohorts meet,
    And on the stormy flood;

Wherever Mammon plants his throne,
  Or mad Ambition reigns;
Wherever Pleasure spreads her zone,
  Or Poverty complains.

O may we hearken to Thy call,
  From ev'ry ill to flee,
And leaving pleasure, wealth and all,
  Arise and follow Thee.

ST. MICHAEL AND ALL ANGELS.

"Are they not all ministering spirits, sent forth to minister for them who shall be heirs of salvation?" HEB. i. 14.

WE are not left alone
To run this mortal race;
The angels of the Lord
Who look upon his face
Are near us, though unseen,
To guide our feet aright;
And, when with sins beset,
To speed us in our flight.

They compass us around,
To do the Lord's behest,
And lead us by the hand,
To safety and to rest;
They comfort us in pain,
They guard us night and day,
And in the hour of death
They bear our souls away.

When shall we meet the saints,
And with the Lord sit down,
And with the angels share
The never-failing crown?
The prize before us set
Is bursting on the sight,
" All angels cry aloud "
Around the throne of light.

Press on, press on! and look
To Jesus at the goal,
The joy before us set
Shall satisfy the soul;

O Lord, Thy will be done,
As in the realms above,
That with the angels, we
May share Thy light and love.

ST. MICHAEL AND ALL ANGELS.

"Take heed that ye despise not one of these little ones, for I say unto
you, that in heaven their angels do always behold the face of my Father
which is in heaven." ST. MATTH. xviii. 10.

GUARDIAN angels, at our birth,
By Thee, O Lord, are giv'n,
Who, while they minister on earth,
Behold Thy face in heav'n.

Guardian angels, when we stray,
Our wand'ring steps restrain ;
Sword-arm'd they meet us on the way,
And turn us back again.

15

Guardian angels, while we sleep,
   Encamp around the scene ;
And silently their vigils keep,
   The earth and heav'n between.

Guardian angels, when we die,
   Our deathless spirits bear
To their retreat within the sky,
   And then enthrone them there.

Scenes of woe and hours of pain,
   Our guardian angels share ;
With them we join th' enraptur'd strain ;
   They strengthen us in pray'r.

Help us do Thy blessed will,
   O Father, Saviour, Friend ;
That we, with holy angels still,
   Th' eternal age may spend.

171

ST. LUKE THE EVANGELIST.

"The harvest truly is great, but the laborers are few: pray ye therefore the Lord of the harvest, that he will send forth laborers into His harvest." ST. MATTH. ix. 37, 38.

The fields of earth are whiten'd o'er,
　And with the harvest bend;
To reap their fruits from shore to shore,
　Thy chosen lab'rers send.

Send them away the lost to search,
　With energy divine,
And gather to Thy ransom'd Church,
　The gleanings of Thy vine.

Be present with them ev'rywhere,
　And guide them from above,
Thy sacred counsels to declare,
　And speak Thy truth in love.

And make them workmen unasham'd,
　When gathering time shall come;
And crown them with the hosts unblam'd,
　At Thy great Harvest-home!

ST. SIMON AND ST. JUDE.

"I heard the voice of the Lord, saying, Whom shall I send, and who will go for us ?   Then said I, here am I, send me."   ISAIAH, vi. 8.

To farthest Ind the trump is blown,
  The banner is unfurl'd ;
The signals to assault the throne
  Of Satan and the world.

" *Whom shall I send, and who will go,*"
  To break their strong-holds down ?
Who, arm'd by God, will meet the foe,
  And wear the victor's crown ?

O may a thousand tongues reply,
  " *Here, Lord, am I, send me,*"
And weapon'd by the Lord Most High,
  Go forth to victory.

Not for the warrior's earthly fame ;
  Not for the crown of pride ;
But far to spread the Word and Name
  Of Christ the Crucified !

The glorious name of God is strong,
.The Word of God is sure;
His Kingdom let the nations throng,
And evermore endure.

ALL SAINTS' DAY. No. 1.

"Make them to be numbered with Thy saints, in glory everlasting."
THE TE DEUM.

PRAISE to the Lord, for saints who rest
From all their toils, among the blest;
The odor of whose sacred lives,
From age to age, the Church revives.

Though dead, they teach Thy perfect ways;
Though silent, they resound Thy praise;
They teach *us* by their patient strife,
They *praise Thee* in their endless life.

Their deeds of faith by thousands sung,
Like incense from the censer flung,
Inspire the living saints to prove
Their work and labor wrought in love.

15*

And glorious is that living band,
Whose feet upon the mountains stand;
Whose voices to the world proclaim
Salvation, in Messiah's name.

In one communion both are blest,
In painful toil or perfect rest;
In heav'n Thy glory *they* display,
We live on earth to watch and pray.

Thy prophets and apostles, Lord,
Make the examples of Thy Word;
Teach us like them our toils to bear;
Make us like them Thy rest to share.

ALL SAINTS' DAY. No. 2.

" Wherefore, seeing we also are compassed about with so great a cloud
of witnesses, let us lay aside every weight and the sin which doth so easily beset us, and let us run with patience the race that is set before us,
looking unto Jesus the Author and Finisher of our faith, &c."

HEB. xii. 1, 2.

O KING of saints, with hearts elate,
We meet the chosen band,

Who round Thy throne of glory wait,
 Redeem'd from ev'ry land ;
The thousands sealèd with Thy name,
Who cloth'd in white, and wing'd with flame,*
 Obey their Lord's command.

Cloud-like they compass us around,
 A bright and countless throng,
And make the place as holy ground,
 In fellowship of song ;
With all, who, 'neath the altar stones,
Cease not to cry in suppliant tones,
 " Holy and True, how long ? "†

The saints who to their rest have fled,
 Who in the Lord have died ;
The crownèd martyrs who have bled,
 And many a one beside ;
Prophets and kings, the wise and great,
Who swell His retinue of state,
 Whom sinful men denied.

  * Psalm, civ. 4.   † Rev. vi. 10.

To their imperial abode,
   They beckon us to rise,
To tread the pathway they have trode,
   And meet them in the skies;
To " walk by faith and not by sight,"
To look to Jesus in the light,
   The light which never dies.

They guide and guard our erring steps,
   They watch around our bed,
And fill the space that intercepts
   The living and the dead.
O speed the time when we shall meet,
And find our fellowship complete,
   In Christ, our living Head !

PART II.

SONGS OF THE CHURCH

FOR

HOLY SOLEMNITIES.

" Ye shall have a Song, as when a holy solemnity is kept ; and gladness of heart, as when one goeth with a pipe to come into the mountain of the Lord, to the Mighty One of Israel."

ISAIAH, xxx. 29.

THE HOLY COMMUNION.

"This do in remembrance of me." St. Luke, xxii. 19.

WITH rapture deep we turn our eyes,
O Lord, upon Thy mysteries;
And in awaken'd mem'ry share
The tender love revealèd there.

And was it not enough to prove,
By dying, Thy undying love?
Or could our ransom'd souls forget
The price, or disavow the debt?

Alas! O Lord, Thou knowest well
The faithless hearts that in us dwell;
How prone to faint, how apt to roam
From paths of duty and from home.

Recall our thoughts to things above,
By this memorial of Thy love;
And, through our faith, by pow'r divine,
Thyself with us in one combine.

16

Pour out Thy Spirit, loving Lord,
And let Thy presence grace the Board,
That all, who seek Thy heav'nly food,
May banquet on Thy flesh and blood.

KNEELING AT THE HOLY COMMUNION.

" Whereas it is ordained in the office for the Administration of the Lord's
Supper, that the Communicants should receive the same *kneeling*," &c.
DECLARATION AT THE END OF THE COMMUNION SERVICE.

To Thee, O Lord, our contrite hearts ascend,
Where Thou enthronèd art in heav'n above,
And when before Thy altar-steps we bend,
It is in adoration of Thy love.

We do no homage to the outward sign,
We yield no worship to the Bread and Wine,
As though Thou wast incorporate therein,
And offer'd there a sacrifice for sin.

We bring to Thee, the sacrifice of praise,
Our souls and bodies for an off'ring meet,
And when to heav'n our grateful hearts we
        raise,
We prostrate fall before Thy mercy-seat.

Before Thy face we cannot stoop too low,
Our deep humility and love to show;
In language high enough we cannot tell
The hope and joy that in Thy myst'ries dwell.

We *stand* t' avouch the Lord to be our God;
We *bow* in rev'rence to His saving name;
Prepar'd to follow in the path He trod,
Prepar'd to share His glory and His shame.

O Jesus, Lord, Thy saving grace impart,
And with devotion fill the contrite heart;
Our forms pervade with piety divine,
And make our worship to resemble Thine.

HOLY BAPTISM.

"Repent, and be baptized every one of you in the name of Jesus Christ,
for the remission of sins, and ye shall receive the gift of the Holy Ghost.
For the promise is unto you, and to your children, and to all that are afar
off, even as many as the Lord our God shall call." ACTS, ii. 38, 39.

BORN to a world of sin and woe,
An heritage of shame;
'T is sweet 'midst changing scenes to know,
Thou, Jesus, art the same.

'T is sweet to know Thy promised love
  Is to our children given ;
With all the signs and means to prove
  Inheritance in heav'n.

'T is sweet, before the sacred Font
  To take the Sponsor's place,
And know Thou wilt, as Thou art wont,
  Pour out Thy saving grace.

Buried with Thee, then cloth'd anew,
  With Thee to life we rise ;
Planted like Thee, with likeness true,
  We meet Thee in the skies.*

And as the sacred waters flow,
  Illume the heav'n above ;
And round the precious off'ring throw
  The shadows of the Dove.†

* Rom. vi. 4, 5.   † Matth. iii. 16.

THE SIGN OF THE CROSS IN HOLY BAPTISM.

"But God forbid that I should glory, save in the Cross of our Lord
Jesus Christ, by whom the world is crucified unto me and I unto the
world." GAL. vi. 14.

THE Cross! the Cross! (the scorner's jest),
On which my Saviour deign'd to die,
I bear it in my secret breast,
I watch it with my gladden'd eye.

The Cross! the Cross! with all its shame,
I cherish on the field and flood;
Inscribèd with Immanuel's name,
And stainèd with his precious blood.

'T was sign'd upon my infant brow,
T' enlist me for the world above:
And shall I fail to own it, now
That I can comprehend its love!

Above the temple spire it shines,
The emblem of the Lord who died;
And to the careless world designs
To teach and preach the Crucified.

16*

In ev'ry scene that meets my view,
In ev'ry thought that stirs within,
O let the Cross my soul subdue,
And keep me from the paths of sin.

All earthly things I count but loss,
And bind myself, O Lord, to Thee,
And in the power of Thy Cross
The world is crucified to me.

CATECHISM.* No. 1.

"Suffer the little children to come unto me, and forbid them not ; for of such is the Kingdom of God." St. Mark, x. 14.

WHILE Thy redeem'd, in realms above,
With angels chant Thy matchless love,
Bow down Thine ear, O Lord, and deign
To fold us to Thine arms again.

* This and the following Hymn may be used in National and Sunday Schools.

O never let us cease to greet
The welcome from Thy mercy-seat,
And make us whom Thy lips shall bless,
The pattern, still, of righteousness.

O take Thy Word, with wisdom fraught,
Engraft it on the bud of thought,
And through its op'ning folds distil
The knowledge of Thy perfect will.

Our hearts reclaimèd, we resign; *
Take them and make them wholly Thine,
That we may live before Thy face,
And walk in truth, and grow in grace.

O let Thy precepts be our guide,
And guard us lest our footsteps slide ;
Let Thy Good Spirit dwell within,
And keep us from the ways of sin.

And as our years with swiftness flee,
Confirm our faith, O Christ, in Thee ;
That we may, when our work is done,
Share the salvation Thou hast won.

* My son, give me thine heart. Prov. xxiii. 26.

CATECHISM. No. 2.

"Out of the mouths of babes and sucklings Thou hast perfected praise." St. Matth. xxi. 16.

Hosanna! once the children's strain,*
  The Prince of Peace to greet;
Hosanna! Lord, the song again,
  Of welcome, we repeat.

Lord, out of weakness comes the strong,
  At Thy divine decree;†
O let Thy grace inspire our song,
  And make it meet for Thee.

Implant Thy Word upon the heart,
  And teach us how to pray,
That we may choose that " *better part*,"
  That passes not away.

And as Thy Holy Spirit strives,
  May we improve our days,
That with our lips and in our lives
  We still may perfect praise.

* Matth. xxi. 15.   † 2 Cor. xii. 9.

Then gently lead us by the hand,
As children of Thy care,
Until we reach the promis'd land,
And sing Hosanna there.

CONFIRMATION.

"Then laid they their hands on them, and they received the Holy Ghost." ACTS. viii. 17.

CALL'D by Thy Word, O Lord,
Before Thy throne we bow,
And in the presence of Thy Church,
Record our solemn vow.

The cross upon our brow,
Has mark'd us for Thine own ;
Thee we confess, and Thee we serve,
The Lord our God, alone.

True to our aim, though weak,
We for Thy succor plead ;
Pour out, we pray, Thy saving strength,
And help us in our need.

To Thee, O Saviour Lord,
Our hearts, our all, we yield;
O make us in Thy service true,
Thy servants call'd and seal'd.*

THE SOLEMNIZATION OF MATRIMONY.   No. 1.

"And both Jesus was called, and his disciples, to the marriage."
ST. JOHN, ii. 2.

JESUS, although there rests the ban,
On stainèd earth and fallen man,
One ray of light we still retain,
To soothe the woe and gild the chain.

One source of bliss where all is pure,
On which Thy blessing rests secure;
One hallow'd state, ordain'd to be
The emblem of Thy Church and Thee.†

* " The ancients called Confirmation, the Sealing of the Spirit."
BISHOP JEREMY TAYLOR.
† Eph. v. 31, 32.

O Saviour, once the welcome guest,
By whom the nuptial feast was blest,
When, yielding to the pow'r divine,
" The water blush'd and turn'd to wine ; "

Thy presence now once more reveal,
Our joys to bless, our vows to seal ;
Extend to us Thy grace, and give
The pow'r in holy love to live ;

That when the cry at Thy return,
Is made, our lamps may brightly burn ;
From watching and from toil set free,
To join Thy train and sup with Thee.

THE SOLEMNIZATION OF MATRIMONY.   No 2.

" It is not good that man should be alone."   Gen. ii. 18.

When Time was young, and man was pure,
  And Eden smil'd serene ;
Ere Satan spread his fatal lure,
  Or aught disturb'd the scene ;

When rais'd, all earthly things above,
　　And near the mercy-seat,
Man needed only woman's love,
　　To make his bliss complete.

And while amidst the toil and care
　　Of this sad world we live,
It sweetens life, the help to share,
　　That woman's love can give.

Affianc'd now, O gracious Lord,
　　Thy thankful servants wait,
And crave the promise of Thy Word
　　To bless the marriage state.

United by Thy firm decree,
　　Let nought the tie divide,
Till they have pass'd this troublous sea,
　　And triumph'd o'er its tide ;

Till they have reach'd *that* scene of bliss,
　　From earthly bonds set free ;
And all the joys that compass *this*,
　　Are ever lost in Thee.

VISITATION OF THE SICK. No. 1.

'And as many as touched Him were made perfectly whole.''
MATTH. xiv. 36.

My heart is smitten down with grief,
   With thoughts of sin oppress'd ;
O Lord, in mercy send relief,
   For I am sore distress'd.

The world in vain exhausts its art,
   In pleasure and in gain ;
It cannot draw the barbèd dart,
   It cannot soothe the pain.

In ev'ry shape my sins appear,
   And on the mem'ry low'r ;
And, charg'd with sorrow and with fear,
   Fill ev'ry waking hour.

Thou, Lord, alone, with pard'ning love
   Canst still the strife within ;
Thy healing touch alone remove
   The weight and pow'r of sin.

17

Look only on my longing soul,
  And all my fears shall cease ;
Speak but the potent word, " *Be whole,*"
  And I shall go in peace.

And henceforth to Thy Word I 'll cling,
  And onward press to heav'n,
To join the thousands there, who sing
  The much Thou hast forgiv'n.*

VISITATION OF THE SICK. No. 2.

" Be still and know that I am God." PSALM xlvi. 10.

Low bending to Thy blessed will,
  I meekly kiss the rod ;
Responsive to the word, " *Be still,*
  And know that I am God."

* St. Luke, vii. 42.

Whate'er Thy sacred will ordain,
　That will, O Lord, be done ;
Why should a living man complain,
　Or wish that will to shun ?

1 know it is my Father's care,
　And feel His promise sure,
That He will give me strength to bear,
　And firmness to endure.

No murm'ring word my lips shall taint,
　Or mingle with my plea ;
And, though my flesh and heart shall faint,
　My trust shall be in Thee.

Whatever be my suff'ring state,
　Amidst severest ill,
O give me grace in faith to wait,
　Thy purpose to fulfil.

Soon the sad night will pass away,
　And sorrow be withdrawn,
And joy and gladness shed their ray
　Upon the opening morn.

COMMUNION OF THE SICK.

"Draw nigh unto God, and He will draw nigh unto you."
St. James, iv. 8.

I MOURN not, for I am not left
Alone, to stem affliction's tide;
I cannot be of joy bereft,
While Thou, O God, art by my side.

Thy presence cheers my silent room,
And soothes me through the weary night;
Thy smile is gladsome 'midst the gloom,
And turns my darkness into light.

Fain would I lift my aching head,
And in Thy temple make my rest;
Before Thine altar break the bread,
And take the cup which Thou hast blest.

O love, beyond expression great,
To spread Thy table near my bed, .
And send Thy ministers to wait
With pow'r to comfort in Thy stead.

Dear at all times, *now* doubly dear,
The emblems of Thy Cross and grave;
O may my soul by faith draw near,
To share the bliss which angels crave.

Once more at love's unfailing spring,
I 'll taste its sweetness ere I die;
Then hasten, with an angel's wing,
To banquet in Eternity.

BURIAL OF THE DEAD. No. 1.

"Weep ye not for the dead, neither bemoan him." Jer. xxii. 10.

No longer for the righteous weep;
They are not dead, but safely sleep
 Beneath the cold damp sod:
And He, who gave them vital breath,
Will keep alive their souls in death,
 The Everlasting God.

Mourn not the man of toil, whose sun
Is set serene, whose work is done,
 Who waits th' expected Lord;
17*

He comes at eventide, to bless
The work and fruit of righteousness,
 With the desired reward.

O let thy cry be calm and brief,
And moan not those with hopeless grief,
 Who to the grave are fled;
The soldier when the strife is done,
The wrestler when the race is run,
 There make their quiet bed.

"O make not much ado nor weep,"*
Thy friends belov'd in Jesus sleep,
 And soon again shall wake;
But wait in faith, and watch and pray,
Until the Everlasting Day
 On thee and them shall break.

Better with Christ to be in peace,
Where tears are not, and troubles cease,
 Beyond all strife and fear;
Better to share His throne on high,
And live beneath His beaming eye,
 Than longer tarry here.

    * Mark, v. 39.

BURIAL OF THE DEAD. No. 2.

"The Lord gave, and the Lord hath taken away ; blessed be the name of the Lord." Job, i. 21.

WITH stricken hearts, before Thy throne
  We meekly kiss the rod,
For love is in Thy judgments shown ;
  " We know that Thou art God."

All things, O Father, come of Thee,
  And bounteous love display,
Nor less of love is Thy decree
  To take these things away.

The loving friends that on us smile,
  To gladden life design'd,
Are only lent us for awhile,
  And then to be resign'd.

We look beyond sepulchral gloom,
  To brighter scenes on high,
Where sweet affections ever bloom,
  And lov'd ones never die ;

Beyond the reach of chance or change,
  No more with sin oppress'd ;
No fightings there our peace derange,
  No fears disturb our rest ;

When all the dead in Christ shall rise,
  To fill the courts above,
And swell the anthem of the skies,
  Re-cloth'd with light and love.

BURIAL OF THE DEAD. No. 3.

"For we must needs die, and are as water spilt on the ground, which
cannot be gathered up again ; neither doth God respect any person : yet
doth He devise means, that His banished be not expelled from Him."

                               2 Sam. xiv. 14.

LIKE water spilt upon the ground,
Soon shall our place no where be found ;
Life, like the fleeting shade of day,
Without impression flits away.

We needs must die; the stern decree
We own, O Lord, and worship Thee;
To Thee we owe our vital breath,
And, trusting Thee, submit to death.

Although we fondly cling to earth,
Our death is better than our birth;
Better with Jesus to appear,
Than in distress to tarry here.

Though banish'd this proscribèd place,
'T is no exclusion from Thy face;
For Thy devisèd means are plain,
*To live is Christ, to die is gain.**

Now while we live, Thy grace impart,
And stamp Thine image on the heart,
That when on earth that day shall break,
We may, like Thee, to glory wake.

* Philip. i. 21.

BURIAL OF THE DEAD AT SEA.

"And the sea gave up the dead which were in it." Rev. xx. 13.

Although no friends were near,
To watch thy dying breath
And weep upon thy bier,
Thy Saviour in his pow'r was nigh,
To hear and grant thy suppliant cry;
And angels watch'd thy death.

The scenes of troubled life
Awaken no alarm;
To thee, though storms are rife,
Though tempests rend the frowning sky,
And ocean fling her waves on high,
The wind and sea are calm.

The fathomless profound
Shall be thy quiet bed;
There rest, until the sound
Through all the ocean-caves shall ring,
The summons of thy God and King,
"*O sea, give up thy dead.*"

CHURCHING OF WOMEN.

"Notwithstanding, she shall be saved in child-bearing." 1 Tim. ii. 15.

When overwhelm'd with fear and grief,
　And threaten'd with despair,
From Thee, O Lord, I sought relief,
　On Thee I cast my care.

Thy promises, like healing balm,
　Were soothing to my pain,
And now, deliver'd by Thine arm,
　I seek Thy courts again.

To health Thy hand hath rais'd me up,
　Thy Word hath made me strong,
And I will take salvation's cup
　And make Thy name my song.

To pleasure Thou hast turn'd my pain,
　My sorrow into joy,
And in Thy service I would fain
　My future life employ.

O take my child and make (*him*) Thine,
    Baptize (*him*) from above;
And fit (*him*) by Thy grace divine,
    To dwell in light and love.

THE COMMINATION.

"And all the people shall answer and say, Amen."*   DEUT. xxvii. 15.

O LIVING God, in this sad hour,
We pray not that Thy dreadful pow'r
    On sinners may alight;
But Thou hast said that wrath shall burn
Upon the soul that will not turn:
    And what Thou say'st is right.

Amen! Amen! we will not shrink
(Whate'er a sinful world may think)
    Thy counsel to declare;
But with uplifted hands we pray,
From sinners turn Thy wrath away,
    And save them from despair.

* Rubric in Commination Service.

Restrain Thine anger, Living God,
And smite not with th' avenging rod,
  Thy self-condemnèd foes ;
Let not Thy dreadful pent up wrath,
With ruin fall upon their path,
  Who Thy sure word oppose.

And send Thy mercy, Gracious King,
On us, who to Thy altar bring
  Affiance in Thy Son :
And sweet, through our unending days,
Shall be the off'ring of our praise :
  Amen ! Thy will be done.

THE DAY OF HER MAJESTY'S ACCESSION. No. 1.

LORD, from Thy throne look down,
And with Thy favor crown
  Our gracious Queen :
18

Extend her peaceful reign,
And ev'ry heart constrain
To join the sacred strain,
  God save the Queen!

On her Thy bounty pour,
And to us evermore
  Thy love increase:
O cause the Light divine
On ev'ry realm to shine,
Till all the earth combine
  To live in peace.

Preserve her sceptre's sway,
And teach us to obey
  Our rightful Queen;
And nations far and nigh,
'Neath Thy approving eye,
Shall swell the anthem high,
  God save the Queen!

THE DAY OF HER MAJESTY'S ACCESSION. No. 2.

GREAT God, upon our native land
   Thy wonted favor send,
For in the strength of Thy right hand
   For safety we depend.

'T is not the tow'rs that line our coast,
   Nor legions of the brave;
'T is not the arm of flesh, we boast
   As powerful to save.

'T is Thou, and not the sword and spear,
   On whom our hopes rely;
'T is Thou, whom arm'd battalions fear,
   Before whose face they fly.

Our princes rule by Thy decree,
   'T is Thine to guard the throne;
Thy word shall make our people free,
   Servants to Thee alone.

In vain the foe our homes assail,
  While shielded by Thine arm;
Against us shall no pow'r prevail,
  ‚No weapon do us harm.

Though hosts of men upon us press,
  We neither faint nor fall,
But armèd with Thy righteousness,
  We triumph over all.

To Thee, O Captain, Saviour, King,
  Our Tow'r of Strength and Shield,
The tribute of our praise we bring,
  To Thee our service yield.

THE DAY OF HER MAJESTY'S ACCESSION. No. 3.

  O KING of Kings, look down,
  And shield us with Thy hand,
  And with Thy favor crown
  Our own, our native land.

Thy guardian care alone
Can keep us from alarm,
Can firmly fix the throne,
And shelter us from harm.

The nations rise to fame,
And empires fall away ;
But Thou art still the same,
Thy reign is endless day.

Thy grace shall make us pure,
Thy truth shall make us free ;
Thy strength our land secure ;
Salvation is of Thee !

18*

THE MAKING, ORDERING AND CONSECRATING OF BISHOPS, PRIESTS, AND DEACONS.

" As my Father hath sent me, so send I you. And when Jesus had said this, He breathed on them and saith unto them, Receive ye the Holy Ghost," &c.—St. John, xx. 21, 22.

Direct, O Lord, Thy Church aright,
Espouse her cause, confirm her call,
And fill them with Thy living light,
On whom the awful lot shall fall.

Be silent now the choice is made,
While on the chosen hands are laid,
While breath'd on, the elected host
Are sealèd with the Holy Ghost.

O consecrate with grace divine
The pow'rs they wield at Thy decree,
And let their embassy be Thine,
To reconcile the world to Thee.

Make them as serpents wise; in love
Let their resemblance be the Dove;
And let no spot of sin deface
The word and ministry of grace.

O Saviour, be forever nigh,
In ev'ry scene, at ev'ry hour
With gifts of grace Thy saints supply,
And crown their work of faith with pow'r.

Add to Thy Church a countless host,
Replenish'd by the Holy Ghost;
And make each ransom'd soul a gem
In their unfading diadem.

THE CHURCH ON THE SEA. No. 1.

" Then He arose and rebuked the winds and the sea: and there was a great calm." St. Matth. viii. 26.

Afloat upon the ocean's breast,
    Lord of the earth and sea;
Where'er we roam, where'er we rest,
    Our hearts are turn'd to Thee.

When o'er the sunlit deep, the sail
    Upon its shadow sleeps,
Or bending with the favoring gale
    Our gallant vessel leaps;

Or when, beneath the flaming sky,
　The clouds are fleet and dark,
And the wild waves are dashing high
　Against our reeling bark;

Thy presence, Lord, is ever nigh,
　Thy promise ever sure,
In troublous times to hear our cry
　And teach us to endure.

Thy presence is our guard from ill,
　Thy promise from alarm;
The word goes forth, the winds are still,
　The angry sea is calm.

We know Thy gentle voice, "'*Tis I*,"
　And feel from danger free;
O save us, Lord, we cannot die,
　While we believe in Thee.

THE CHURCH ON THE SEA. No. 2.

"And they that were in the ship came and worshipped Him, saying, Of truth Thou art the Son of God." St. Matth. xiv. 33.

THE temple of the Lord Most High
  We make this lofty dome —
Its canopy, the arching sky,
  Its floor, the ocean's foam.

Deep, calling to the answering deep,
  Is vocal with a song,
And the wild waves that o'er us sweep,
  The rapt'rous strain prolong.

Our altar is the rolling deck,
  As on our course we fly,
Or on the fragment of the wreck
  When stranded deep we lie.

Far from the land which gave us birth
  The home of early love ;
Cut off from all our friends on earth,
  We look to One above :

Our Friend and Father, who controls
   The earth, the sea and sky;
" The Son of God," on whom our souls
   In confidence rely.

We need not fear when Thou art nigh;
   Thine arm salvation brings:
We cannot perish, while we lie
   Beneath Thy shelt'ring wings.

THE CHURCH IN EXILE.

" If we walk in the light as He is in the light, we have fellowship one
with another." 1 JOHN, i. 7.

THOUGH far across the western main,
   In other lands we roam,
No space can break the mystic chain
   Which binds us to our home.

Our friends, although unseen, we greet ;
  Though silent, they are heard,
When walking in the light we meet,
  And speak our mother's word.*

One saving faith in which we stand,
  One Lord on whom we call,
One Bread to break at His command,
  One Baptism for all.

Although in body far apart,
  In spirit we are one ;
O Saviour, knit each kindred heart,
  Until our work be done.

And still our fellowship prolong,
  When made complete in Thee ;
One heart, one voice, one glorious song,
  To fill Eternity !

* "To the emigrant far removed from home and friends, the Book of
Common Prayer is unspeakably precious, the firm and lasting tie, when
all other ties are snapped." SOUTHEY.

THE CHURCH IN THE CAMP. No. 1.

"Jehovah-shalom." Judges, vi. 24.

At war, and on the tented field,
Thou art, O Lord, our strength and shield;
To Thee, in all our straits, we fly,
And on Thy conqu'ring arm rely.

By foemen challeng'd to the fight,
We go to battle in Thy might,
And when before our face they flee,
The conquest we ascribe to Thee.

O speed the time when strife shall cease,
And love resume a reign of peace,
And ev'ry hostile land shall sing
The Psalm of Peace to God our King.

Thou, Prince of Peace, to all the world
O let Thy standard be unfurl'd;
Thy promis'd Kingdom soon restore,
Where we may live and war no more.

THE CHURCH IN THE CAMP. No. 2.

"Jehovah-Nissi." Exodus, xvii. 15.

To arms! to arms! the battle cry
   Rings forth its baleful notes,
And, in defiance lifted high,
   The hostile standard floats.

In Thee we trust, and fear no harm,
   " Lord of all pow'r and might " ;
With Thy right hand and holy arm,
   Thou wilt defend the right.

To arms! to arms! the trumpets sound
   The summons to the field ;
Our God is on the embattl'd ground,
   Our Banner and our Shield.

Thine is the battle, mighty King,
   O save us from defeat,
And all our trophies we will bring,
   And cast them at Thy feet.

19

To arms! to arms! O Lord forgive,
  And saving grace supply;
If spar'd — to Christ we henceforth live;
  If slain — 't is gain to die!

THE CHURCH IN TIME OF WARS AND TUMULTS. No. 1.

"When the host goeth forth against thine enemies, then keep thee from every wicked thing." DEUT. xxiii. 9.

THE ruthless foe, with iron hand,
In deadly strife hath drawn the brand;
The torch of discord, flaming high,
Shoots its wild light afar and nigh;
And War, with all its threat'ning train,
O'erspreads the blighted earth again.

Our sins provoke Thy wrath, O Lord,
Our crying sins unsheathe the sword:
But we repent: — Thy wrath restrain —
With favor turn to us again —
And on the battle flood and field,
Be Thou our succor and our shield.

Gird on Thy sword, O Lord of might,
Guard us and teach our hands to fight;
Teach us on Thee our hope to stay,
That when our foes shall flee away,
Our tongues may tell, in thankful songs,
To Thee alone the praise belongs.

Thy kingdom come, when wars shall cease
Within Thy realm, O Prince of Peace!
When diff'ring tribes Thy sceptre own,
And meet in concord round Thy throne;
And love extend its influence bland
To ev'ry heart in ev'ry land.

THE CHURCH, IN TIME OF WARS AND TUMULTS. No. 2.

"Pray for the peace of Jerusalem." PSALM cxxii. 6.

O SAVIOUR, from Thy throne on high,
Look down on earth with pitying eye;
Put up the sword, for field and flood
Are crimson'd o'er with human blood.

The widow's wail, the orphan's prayer,
The childless mother's wild despair,
And peaceful homes in ruin laid,
Proclaim the havoc war has made.

If triumph come, its baleful tread
Is o'er the warrior's gory bed,
'Midst painèd cries and dying throes,
Of victor friends and vanquish'd foes.

Once more, command the storm to cease,
And let the earth repose in peace ;
Once more, the wrath of man restrain,
And turn it to Thy praise again.*

O let Thy Church " *arise and shine,*"
To fill the world with love divine ;
Extend Thy truth from shore to shore,
And war shall vex the earth no more.

* Psalm lxxvi. 10.

THE CHURCH IN PLAGUE OR PESTILENCE.

"God is our Refuge and Strength, a very present help in trouble."

IN grief and fear, to Thee, O Lord,
  We now for succor fly,
And while Thy judgments are abroad,
  O shield us, lest we die.

The fell disease on ev'ry side
  Walks forth, with tainted breath;
And Pestilence, with rapid stride,
  Bestrews the land with death.

Our sins Thy dreadful anger raise,
  Our deeds Thy wrath deserve;
But we repent, and from Thy ways
  We never more will swerve.

O look with pity on the scene
  Of sadness and of dread,
And let Thy angel stand between
  The living and the dead.

19*

With contrite hearts, to Thee, our King,
  We turn, who oft have stray'd;
Accept the sacrifice we bring,
  And let the plague be stay'd.*

CONSECRATION OF CHURCHES. No. 1.

"And Jacob awaked out of his sleep, and he said, Surely the Lord is in this place; and I knew it not. And he was afraid and said, How dreadful is this place! this is none other but the house of God, and this is the gate of Heaven." GEN. xxviii. 16, 17.

O GOD of glory and of grace,
Whose presence fills all time and space,
  Unlimited art Thou:
Before whose high and radiant throne
Of jasper and the sardine stone,
  The holy angels bow.

All we possess, O Lord, is Thine;
Then come, and with Thy pow'r divine,
  This house with glory fill:

* Numbers, xvi. 48, 50.   2 Samuel, xxiv. 25.

O come, and take it for Thine own,
Record Thy name, erect Thy throne,
 And bend us to Thy will.

O Saviour, gather'd in Thy name,
The promise of Thy Word we claim,
 As dew on Gideon's fleece;
The fount of living light unseal,
And to our souls Thyself reveal,
 The Source of life and peace.

'T is good to feel Thy presence near,
'T is good Thy still small voice to hear
 In Zion's lov'd retreat;
And, day by day, with joy prolong
The matin prayer and evening song,
 Before Thy mercy-seat;

And through our life's remaining hours,
To guard its gates and watch its tow'rs,
 And rest its courts within:
Beneath its shade to watch and pray,
Until by angels borne away,
 Beyond the reach of sin.

CONSECRATION OF CHURCHES. No. 2.

WITH foes beset, with fears distress'd,
　Whatever evils come,
Near to the Church we make our rest,
　Within its courts our home.

Although unseen by human eye,
　Unheard by human ear,
'T is *Bethel*, and the Lord Most High
　Is ever present here.

When from temptation's serpent-face,
　We turn to it and flee,
'T is *Bethany*, the house of Grace;
　We reach it, and are free.

And when with thoughts of sin dismay'd,
　The contrite bosom swells,
It is *Bethesda's* scene display'd,
　The house where Mercy dwells.

When on Thy Holy Table spread,
  The Holy Myst'ries lie,
'T is *Bethlehem*, the house of Bread;
  We eat, and never die.

Our safe retreat in ev'ry woe,
  Our banquet-scene of love;
The house of God on earth below,
  The gate of heav'n above.

CONSECRATION OF CHURCHES. No. 3.

" My house shall be called the house of prayer." ST. MATTH. xxi. 13.

To Thee we dedicate this Fane,
  To Thee our off'rings bring,
Whom the wide heav'ns cannot contain,
  O Lord, our God and King.

To Thee all wealth is nothing worth,
  The heav'n of heav'ns to fill;
Much less this temple rear'd on earth,
  And built by mortal skill.

Thy Presence, Lord, pervades all space
   All precious things are Thine;
O write Thy name upon this place,
   With glory fill this shrine.

When in Thy light, we see the light,
   And hear the joyful sound,
Pour through its aisles the halo bright,
   And make it holy ground.

Ope wide its gates, as Thou art wont,
   For Thine elected host,
And let them at the sacred font
   Receive the Holy Ghost.

And when around Thy board to sup,
   We meet at Thy command,
Replenish Thou, with grace, the Cup
   Of Blessing in our hand.

In peace and pardon let us share,
   Till, purg'd of earthly leav'n,
We find within this house of pray'r
   The open gate of heav'n.

STUDENTS OF THE CHURCH.

"Study to shew thyself approved unto God, a workman that needeth not to be ashamed, rightly dividing the word of truth."   2 Tim. ii. 15.

FOUNTAIN of life, in whom the light
   Forever shines serene,
At whose command chaotic night
   Became a radiant scene ; -

Once more let Thy enlight'ning ray
   Thy purposes fulfil,
And to inquiring minds display
   The knowledge of Thy will.

Remove the vail from off the heart,
   The film from off the eyes,
And make us all, who " *know in part*,"
   To Thy salvation wise.

All that we gain of sacred lore,
   The fruit of all research,
To Thee, O Saviour, we restore,
   To serve Thee in Thy Church.

Give us the prophets' mind to learn,
The prophets' mind to teach,
The prophets' wisdom to discern,
The prophets' fire to preach.

Make us like martyrs to forgive,
Like martyrs to forbear;
That we a martyr's life may live,
A martyr's triumph share.

MISSIONARIES OF THE CHURCH.

" And He said unto them, Go ye into all the world, and preach the Gos
pel to every creature." St. MARK, xvi. 15.

BESTOW'D by Thy all-bounteous hand,
All we possess, O Lord, is Thine;
And rising up at Thy command,
That all, we gratefully resign;

To preach the Word, and bear the Cross
Through scenes of sorrow and dismay,
And count all present gains but loss,
That cause our feeble steps to stray.

The home in which our childhood sped,
The friends that round our hearts entwine,
The place where lie our cherish'd dead,
All, all to JESUS we resign.

Within the Church our home is found,
In ev'ry hour, in ev'ry land,
And where the SAVIOUR's poor abound,
Our friends are in their lowly band.

Our hostel, like the desert Isle,*
Where God's pavilion open'd wide,
Is made the scene in which awhile
We wait for light at eventide.

When, having wrought in faith and love,
Our shifting tent is taken down,
We find our resting-place above,
And wear the never-fading crown.

* Patmos.

20

When, changèd in our Easter birth,*
The face of JESUS we behold,
All that we sacrifice of earth
Is recompens'd a hundred fold.†

Redeem'd, and by His love constrain'd,
O may we with the angels vie,
To serve the cause in which He deign'd
To toil, to suffer, and to die.

MISSIONARY SOCIETIES OF THE CHURCH.

WHO for the Saviour, who
Will saving grace proclaim ?
Who to His cause and banner true,
Will spread His glorious name ?

The dew on Gideon's fleece,
Was fire on Gideon's sword,‡
And thoughts of triumph and of peace
Breathe in the living Word.

* Luke, xx. 36.   † Matt. xix. 29.   ‡ Judges, vi. 37.

The dewy Cross once trac'd
Upon our infant brow,
Is not, and cannot be, effac'd :
Afresh it gloweth now.

Up, soldiers of the Cross,
Our banner is unfurl'd ;
Strong in the Lord, whate'er the loss,
We triumph o'er the world.

Soon shall the desert spring
With Eden's flowers again,
And tongues, long mute, with rapture sing
The Lamb's triumphant strain.

And soon, from soul to soul
The saving truth shall run,
And tell to earth, from pole to pole,
Messiah's work is done !

THE CHURCH BELLS.

No sound that greets the early hour,
    Of sabbath rest to tell,
Is like the concert in the Tow'r,
    The music of the Bell.

Above the world's tumultuous din
    It comes, our thoughts to raise,
To string with love the heart within,
    And tune the voice to praise.

And when on sorrow's darken'd scenes,
    Its sweet vibrations break,
Its soothing tones subdue our threnes,
    As though an angel spake.

Blithely it peals for all who share
    The joy of new-blest love,
As if to tell the wedded pair,
    Of sympathy above.*

* "This is a great mystery, but I speak concerning Christ and His Church." Eph. v. 32.

Or when it tolls, with mournful surge,
  Our lov'd ones to dismiss,
It mingles with the funeral dirge,
  The melody of bliss.

I listen to its welcome notes,
  Where'er my footsteps roam ;
When on the passing breeze, it floats,
  And calls me to my home.

In ev'ry hour, in ev'ry clime,
  In ev'ry house we dwell,
No music like the sacred chime,
  The music of the Bell.

THE CHURCH MUSIC.

" Praise Him upon the well-tuned cymbals :   praise Him upon the loud cymbals.   Let every thing that hath breath praise the Lord."
                                                PSALM cl. 5, 6.

It tunes the heart to muse on things above,
It fills the soul with sacred fire of love ;
Refines the thoughts and stills the inward strife,

Which jars the concord of this earthly life.
When touch'd with skill, the organ lifts its
  voice,
And swells the welcome summons to rejoice.

Softly around the aërial music floats,
As though an angel swept its solemn notes,
Or with its choral melody profound,
Pours through the aisles its torrent-tide of
  sound :
As when the hosts seraphic, from on high
In one loud concert blend th' incessant cry.

Its plaintive tones dissolve us into tears,
Now raise our hopes, and now revive our
  fears ;
Now cast us down in sorrow and dismay,
Now bear the soul with rapt'rous joy away,
Where, tun'd to golden harps, the angels
  sing
The never-ceasing anthem to their King.

Praise ye the Lord, with their celestial train,
Lift up your hearts, and emulate their strain ;

Strike the full chords, and make the Church
    rejoice
With well-tun'd cymbals, and her living voice,
Till " *all the company of heaven* " combine
To make her songs eternal and divine.

                  Hosanna !

Check Out More Titles From HardPress Classics Series In this collection we are offering thousands of classic and hard to find books. This series spans a vast array of subjects – so you are bound to find something of interest to enjoy reading and learning about.

Subjects:
Architecture
Art
Biography & Autobiography
Body, Mind &Spirit
Children & Young Adult
Dramas
Education
Fiction
History
Language Arts & Disciplines
Law
Literary Collections
Music
Poetry
Psychology
Science
...and many more.

Visit us at www.hardpress.net

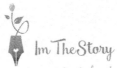

CPSIA information can be obtained
at www.ICGtesting.com
Printed in the USA
BVHW041447140819
555860BV00026B/2340/P